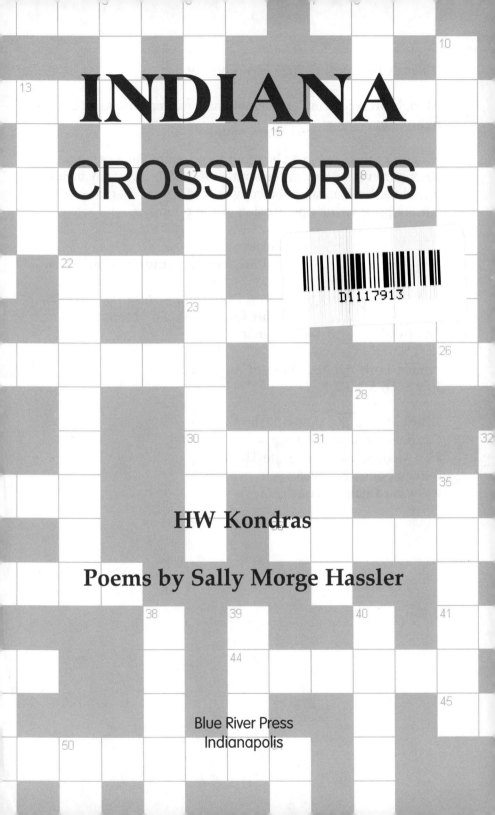

INDIANA

CROSSWORDS

HW Kondras

Poems by Sally Morge Hassler

Blue River Press
Indianapolis

Indiana Crosswords © 2003 HW Kondras

Cover designed by Phil Velikan
Cover photography by Phil Velikan and by Painet.inc
www.painetworks.com
Interior photography by Tom Doherty and Lisa Paczkowski, maps by Phil Velikan, clip art from www.clipart.com.
Proofread by Christopher Stolle

Printed in the United States of America
10 9 8 7 6 5 4 3 2 1

Distributed in the United States by
Cardinal Publishers Group
7301 Georgetown Rd., Suite 118
Indianapolis, IN 46268
www.cardinalpub.com

For the people who have always made Indiana the best place in the world to me: Mom, Dad, Paul and Matthew, Jill and Amara, and especially Bob.

From left to right, Tommy, Makenna and Marissa enjoying a beautiful Indiana winter's day while sledding at Cool Creek Park in Carmel, Indiana.

Table of Contents

Author's Note

Each puzzle features an Indiana topic but not all of the clues will be about the Hoosier state. To clarify when you should be thinking of Indiana answers, I have marked those clues with a "★".

I am deeply indebted to a number of people who helped with this book. Thanks to Laurette McCarthy, Evan Finch, Phil Velikan, Lisa Paczkowski, Jill Erickson, Sally Hassler, Heather Lowhorn, Christopher Stolle and Kim Heusel for their help with the puzzles and in finding the information to put the puzzles together. Thanks to Bob, Jill, Amara, Ewa, Patti, John and Jean and my parents for being supportive while I was working on it, and — last but not least — thanks to Tom Doherty for talking me into doing it in the first place.

I hope you have as much fun working on the puzzles as I had writing them.

ABE IN INDIANA
by Sally Morge Hassler

Walking from Kentucky
To chop Indiana wood
And help build a one-room cabin,
Came old Abe in boyhood.
At the tender age of seven,
He came to the Hoosier state,
And he stayed for fourteen years
Where he read and wrote on slate.
When he wasn't in the fields
Working with his might,
He was borrowing books
To read by candlelight.
At the age of twenty-one,
Abe moved on to Illinois,
But Indiana is proud
That she raised him from a boy.

INDIANA
PEOPLE
"Hoosiers"

What is a Hoosier?

Well, there are a lot of theories as to how the name came about, ranging from the silly ("It's what people from Indiana say when you knock on their door: 'Who's 'ere?') to the plausible (the foreman for the workers who were in Indiana at the time might have been named "Hoosier," and his employees became known as "Hoosier's men" and then simplified to "Hoosiers"). However, I like to think that being a Hoosier is a state of mind — optimism grounded in common sense, tremendous work ethic combined with an appreciation for good humor and good work of all kinds: art, sport, commerce and handiwork.

There have been many Hoosiers who were great politicians, artists, comedians and business people, and there are sure to be many more in the future. The following puzzles highlight some of the people who have brought the values they learned in Indiana to the world at-large.

1

Hoosier Greats

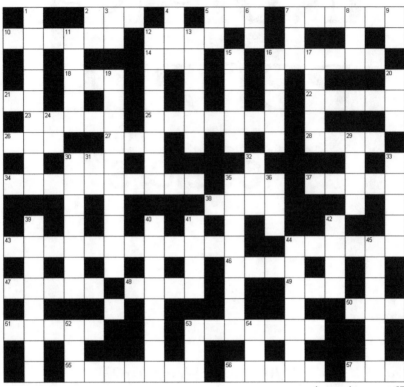

Answer is on page 87

ACROSS

2. Fool
5. Popular conjunction
7. J. Danforth _____, former U.S. Vice President ★
10. Infamous Hoosier Charles _____ was a resident of the Indiana Boys School in Plainfield before escaping in a stolen car to California. ★
12. Gigot
14. The pussycat's wooer
16. Hitchcock film, *Rear* _____
18. _____ and vigor
21. _____ *the Waterfront*
22. Torrent
23. Phonic
25. Amelia _____, the great avatrix, was on leave from Purdue University when she disappeared during an attempted flight around the world. ★
26. What she'll have "til Daddy takes the T-bird away"
27. To fall behind
28. Anno
30. "___ No Evil"

34. Indianapolis native and Pulitzer prize winner Booth _____ wrote *The Magnificent Ambersons* and *Alice Adams*.★

35. An incline of the body to show respect or a ribbon in a child's hair

37. The Big "O", _____ Robinson led Crispus Attucks to state basketball championships in 1955 and 1956.★

38. Evan ____, former governor of Indiana and current senator, simply followed in his father's footsteps.★

43. Basketball legend Stephanie _____ played high school, college and pro ball here in Indiana.★

44. UCLA made him famous, but John _____'s coaching career began at Martinsville High School.★

46. Tropical island paradise

47. Big pebble

48. French Lick ballplayer that brought Indiana State basketball to the national spotlight: Larry ____★

49. Opposite of truth

50. Three Dog Night lyric: "The __ is black; the page is white."

51. The songwriter who brought us "Georgia on My Mind," _____ Carmichael is a Hoosier.★

53. Now known as "The Great One," Wayne _____ played his first 8 pro games for the Indianapolis Racers.★

55. Indiana astronaut Gus _____ was the second man in space.★

56. Infamous Hoosier Jim _____ built a following of believers in Indianapolis before leading them to their deaths in Guyana.★

57. Epoch

DOWN

1. Hoosier Barbara Moore, an arachnid fan, was the founder of the American _____ Society. ★

2. Do, Re, Me, Fa, ___, La, Ti

3. Abbreviation for octane number

4. Many are called, but ____ are chosen.

5. Paul Simon: "You can call me ___."

6. Wedding vow word

7. French for "who?"

8. ___ hoo!

9. French "and"

11. Sandy Allen of Shelbyville was named the tallest living women by the *Guiness Book of Records*. She stood at ___ feet, 7¼ inches tall.★

12. The renowned author of *Slaughterhouse-Five*, Kurt _____ grew up in Indianapolis. ★

13. An IU favorite for his contributions to the 1987 NCAA Championship, this player is now the head coach of Iowa.★

15. The story of this high school team's victory inspired the movie "Hoosiers."★

16. This young AIDS activist from Kokomo was a hero to many: Ryan ____.★

17. Smart, stylish
19. Although he first became famous as "John Cougar," this Seymour native prefers this, his real name.★
20. A sweetened drink made from water and fruit juice
24. Toronto's province (abbrev)
29. Bend
30. This Indiana comedian had a hit television show from 1953 to 1970: Red _____.★
31. Old MacDonald's favorite vowels
32. Flirty-shy, like Marvel's mistress
33. Famous for his landscape paintings, T.C. Steele owned many acres in this scenic Indiana county.★
35. Kenneth Edmonds of Indianapolis, better known by this nickname, is the producer, writer or performer of more than 50 hit songs.★

36. Cindy Lou's last name
39. Hoosier poet, James _____ Riley, was also famous for his little dog, Lockerbie.★
40. George _____ had an outstanding career at Washington High School before becoming a leader for the ABA and NBA Pacers.★
41. Barren
42. This giant word sits in front of the Indianapolis Museum of Art, sculpted by Hoosier Robert Indiana. ★
44. The Republican candidate for president in 1940 was from Elwood, Indiana: Wendell _____.★
45. Dusk
52. A joke
53. Jewel
54. Also

James Whitcomb Riley

One of Indiana's favorite sons, James Whitcomb Riley was one of the most popular poets of the late 19th and early 20th century. He was most famous for his poems for children and for his use of dialect to tell stories, capturing the voice of the midwestern merchant, immigrant farmer or country child as the story dictated. On the following page, you'll find a word search listing the names of some of Riley's most famous poems.

James Whitcomb Riley

```
            Z L P A
            D V N E
            A O J I
        J T G C U H M K R Y
      A N O L D F R I E N D Z G W
     A M A N O F M A N Y P A R T S E
    D N N O N A M Y D E G G A R E H T C
   I L D O O H Y B A B K S T Z O D J Z F X
  L E R T S N I M E H T F O P R A H E H T I X
  R A U L S M K R A L C R M C I R T N E C C E
  Y Q L L A F S W O D A H S G N I N E V E N E H W
  A S X F G B H       Z L U H       Y P O F J G Y
  J T H E R O S E     I D M N     O L A T O O B J
  G H U F A N X F     A S F U     G X K D J W V G
 W H E N T H E F R O S T I S O N T H E P U N K I N R G B
 G U F E Z L I T T L E O R P H A N T A N N I E I L F E X
 N C R S R L Z A J S D N A H L U F I T U A E B R E H T A
 E V O L F O T S E T A S U M M E R A F T E R N O O N S S
 E M G N I L T S I H W Y O B A O T H E M E R M A N U E V
 M A I L L I W R E H T A F A W I L D I R I S H M A N
 N W E E I T   L   V   F   P   Z   T   D   H M D R A
 W J R O B                             E J Y W
 Y R O D J E B A O U R L I T T L E G I R L D Y H
  M G H A N R G S A N E M P T Y N E S T E S W
   C W N Y I T G N V M D C U P A U G U S T E
    Q D W W L D Y R E D R I D I N G H O O D
     J X A N A B A C K W A R D L O O K
      P L L O R D E D L I G E H T
        L S V T M P S V U Y
          H A D E X L
```

A Backward Look	Eccentric Mr. Clark	The Harp of the Minstrel
A Man of Many Parts	Father William	The Merman
A Nest Egg	Her Beautiful Hands	The Raggedy Man
A Summer Afternoon	John Walsh	The Rose
A Summer Sunrise	Liberty	To a Boy Whistling
A Test of Love	Little Orphant Annie	Tradin Joe
A Wild Irishman	Only a Dream	When Evening Shadows Fall
An Empty Nest	Our Little Girl	When the Frost is on the Punkin
An Old Friend	Red Riding Hood	
August	The Frog	
Babyhood	The Gilded Roll	

Answer is on page 88

5

LITTLE ORPHANT ANNIE
by James Whitcomb Riley
Reprinted with the permission of Guild Press

INSCRIBED WITH ALL FAITH AND AFFECTION
To all the little children: — The happy ones; and sad ones;
The sober and the silent ones; the boisterous and glad ones;
The good ones — Yes, the good ones, too; and all the lovely
bad ones.

Little Orphant Annie's come to our house to stay,
An' wash the cups an' saucers up, an' brush the crumbs away,
An' shoo the chickens off the porch, an' dust the hearth, an'
sweep,
An' make the fire, an' bake the bread, an' earn her board-an-
keep;
An' all us other childern, when the supper-things is done,
We set around the kitchen fire an' has the mostest fun,
A-listenin' to the witch-tales 'at Annie tells about,
An' the Gobble-uns 'at gits you
     Ef you
       Don't
         Watch
          Out!

Wunst they wuz a little boy wouldn't say his prayers, —
An' when he went to bed at night, away up-stairs,
His Mammy heerd him holler, an' his Daddy heerd him bawl,
An' when they turn't the kivvers down, he wuzn't there at all!
An' they seeked him in the rafter-room, an' cubby-hole, an' press,
An seeked him up the chimbly-flue, an' ever'-wheres, I guess;
But all they ever found wuz thist his pants an' roundabout: —
An' the Gobble-uns 'll git you
     Ef you
       Don't
         Watch
          Out!

An' one time a little girl 'ud allus laugh an' grin,
An' make fun of ever' one, an' all her blood-an'-kin;
An' wunst, when they was "company," an' ole folks wuz there,
She mocked 'em an' shocked 'em, an' said she didn't care!
An' thist as she kicked her heels, an' turn't to run an' hide,
They wuz two great big Black Things a-standin' by her side,
An' they snatched her through the ceilin' 'for she knowed what
she's about!
An' the Gobble-uns 'll git you
    Ef you
       Don't
         Watch
         Out!

An' little Orphant Annie says, when the blaze is blue,
An' the lamp-wick sputters, an' the wind goes woo-oo!
An' you hear the crickets quit, an' the moon is gray,
An' the lightnin'bugs in dew is all squenched away, —
You better mind yer parunts, an' yer teachurs fond an' dear,
An' cherish them 'at loves you, an' dry the orphant's tear,
An' he'p the pore an' needy ones 'at clusters all about,
Er the Gobble-uns 'll git you
    Ef you
       Don't
         Watch
         Out!

From *Riley Child-Rhymes with Hoosier Pictures* by James Whitcomb Riley with pictures by Will Vawter, available from Guild Press. *The Orphant Annie Story Book* by Johnny Gruelle, the original creator of Raggedy Ann and Andy, was dedicated to the memory of James Whitcomb Riley and opened with this poem. This book is also available from Guild Press of Indiana. To order a copy, please visit their website: www.guildpress.com.

THE HOOSIER POET
by Sally Morge Hassler

If'n I could only be
a poet as good as Riley
It'd make me awful proud you see
to write like Whitcomb Riley
Just think how grand my poems would be
like James Whitcomb Riley.

Born in a two-room cabin
in Greenfield, Indiana,
he wrote a lot about our state
and wrote them poems really great.
It'd make me awful proud you see
to write such Hoosier poetry.

Below: Indiana's tallest Christmas tree with young hoosiers Hannah and Lucy

Hoosier Musicians

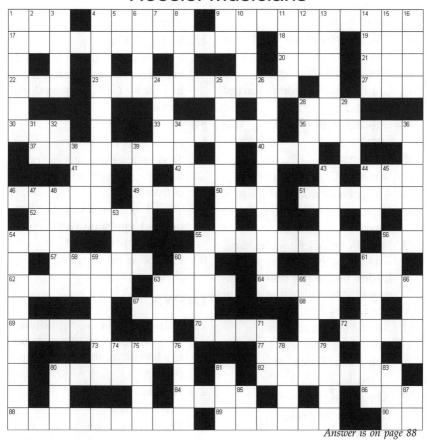

Answer is on page 88

ACROSS

1. James Bond flick: __ *Another Day*
4. Philosopher and author, Albert _____
9. Father-centered society
17. This capital city is the birthplace of legendary bluesman Edward Lamonte Franklin. ✰
18. Who __ you?
19. Country music television: "___-Haw"
20. Big sister in *Little Women*
21. Baseball statistic
22. Convent-dweller
23. His hits include "Jack and Diane," "R.O.C.K. in the U.S.A.," and "Small Town" ✰
27. French iron
28. A small chasm
30. Tasty declaration
33. Bugs Bunny's favorite snack
35. Drummer from "The Muppet Show"

9

37. Band that Bloomington-born David Lee Roth fronted for many years ✳
40. What Robin Hood did to the rich
41. Movie studio (abbrev.)
42. Graduate school admission test (abbrev.)
44. Children's storybook: ___ the Bunny
46. Fancy fur
49. Southern Civil War general
50. Alcohol once made in bath tubs
51. Hometown of country singer Sylvia ✳
52. Phil Harris of Linton, Indiana, was an actor and orchestra leader, but might be most famous for providing the voice of this Disney bear.✳
54. An affirmative answer
55. Jackson who recorded "Let Me Tickle Your Fancy" ✳
56. ___, so, la, ti
57. A beginning (abbrev.)
60. Father, on the prairie
61. Follows re
62. Worried
63. Tarzan's girlfriend
64. Cause of death of Indiana blues legend "Scrapper" Blackwell✳
67. Hoosier singer-actress Florence Henderson's hometown ✳
68. State that's home to the Grand Ole Opry (abbrev.)
69. Superlative
70. Utensil
72. An old-fashioned term for a cleaning woman

73. A combination of smoke and haze
77. Afresh
80. Stoplight: Go
82. Indiana native that was voted one of Nashville's sexiest men in 1992 by *USA Today* readers, Steve ____ ✳
84. Not in danger
86. A space for cats to sit
88. To say something quickly or in a lively manner: a _____ delivery
89. This Hoosier native's first number one song was "Don't Worry 'Bout Me Baby." ✳
90. Can be used to mean "Hey, You!"

DOWN

1. Indiana University graduate Howard Ashman rose to fame as a lyricist for this movie company ✳
2. Not out
3. Eve's garden
4. This Indiana songwriter won an Oscar for "In the Cool, Cool, Cool of the Evening." ✳
5. __ Apple
6. Shopping destination
7. Not down
8. Marilyn Monroe: ___ *Like it Hot*
9. Rounded off, it's 3.14
10. The most populous continent
11. A slope
12. Anger
13. Greek island body of water
14. An expert in food preparation
15. "The buck stops ____."

16. Twelve months
24. Stevie Nicks: "Leather and ___"
25. Indiana jazz great "Eddie" Condon was celebrated at this prestigious New York music hall in an all-star salute in 1972★
26. Music timing devices
28. A smooth talker is said to have "the gift of ___."
29. Something to hold your dress together or the number you need at an ATM
31. Protective coating for glasses
32. Mother, on the prairie
34. Heavenly guardian
36. Jackson who recorded "If You Feel the Funk"★
38. ___ and Void
39. Comic Strip: Little ___
43. Known as "J.J.," this Indianapolis-born musican wrote the score for *Cleopatra Jones* ★
44. Dr. Seuss: someone to hop on
45. Neil Diamond: "I ___, I Said"
47. Name that goes with "honest"
48. Indiana drummer Harold J. Jones joined this musical Count's group in 1967.★
53. Hoosier singer Connie Smith became a member of this country music institution in 1965, The Grand Ole ___ ★

54. A child
55. Jackson who recorded the hit album *Control*★
56. Necessary swimming equipment for a fish
58. It doesn't apply to me (abbrev.)
59. African fly type
60. "My ___ Joey"
61. Member of the Jackson Five whose first solo hit was "Got To Be There" in 1971★
63. Type of music played by Anderson, Indiana, musician Gary Burton★
65. Not you or yours
66. Al or Tipper
71. Rule
74. Who? ___?
75. Against
76. Poise
78. Officer who specialize in drug violations
79. This Indiana native won an Academy Awards for his associations with *The Sound of Music* and *West Side Story*★
80. Trendy casual wear store
81. Not on
83. Madonna: "___ of Light"
85. Must-see-TV medical drama
87. Polonium (abbrev.)

The Hoosier Group

You might be familiar with many of the movies, actors, singers and songwriters that are from Indiana that have been active in the arts for much of the last 50 years, but did you know that Indiana was once on the leading edge in art? The Hoosier Group, made up of TC Steele, Otto Stark, Richard Gruelle, William Forsyth and John Ottis Adams, were seen at the end of the 19th century as the first American artists to show individualtiy of style and showcase a truly American expression within the modern style of painting.

The five painters were exhibited together in 1894 by the Central Art Association in Chicago. The show was described in their catalog as follows:

"To the Art Lovers of Chicago, The Central Art Association takes peculiar pleasure in presenting, as its first special exhibit, the work of five "Hoosier" painters, for aside from their inherent excellence as artists, the history of their development has special sigifigance. It exemplifies all the difficulties in the way of original western art and foreshadows its ultimate victory. These men were isolated from their fellow-artists, they were surrounded by apparently the most unpromising material, yet they set themselves to the task right manfully and this exhibition demonstrates the power of the artist's eye to find floods of color, graceful forms and interesting compositions everywhere. These artists have helped the people of Indiana to see the beauty in their own quiet landscape. They have not only found interesting things to pain in things near at hand; they have made these chosen scenes interesting to others. Therein lies their sigifigance."

Our thanks to art historian Laurette McCarthy for her contribution to this section of the text.

Hoosiers in the Arts

Answer is on page 89

ACROSS

2. When Dorothy _____ wrote a cookbook in 1996, her name appeared on the cover as simply "Dave's Mom." ✷

7. Moby Dick's captain

10. Monkey see, monkey ___

12. Something you keep up your sleeve

14. Holly Hobbie's precocious pig pair: ___ and Puddle

15. Birthplace of Hoosier poet William Herschell✷

17. Home to Hoosier writer Booth Tarkingto.✷

20. Moises and Felipe's surname

21. Audio-Visual (abbrev.)

22. Opposite of yes

23. The Indiana author of *Happy Birthday, Wanda June*✷

24. Auger

26. A Terre Haute native, this author's *Sister Carrie* and *An*

American Tragedy became classics in the category of American realistic fiction. ✶

27. *Alice of Old* _____, written by Hoosier Maurice Thompson, is a historical romance that takes place during the George Rogers Clark expendition. ✶
28. Negative
30. *Much ___ About Nothing*
32. Exist
33. Harol Reed Langland created the statue called "Christ _____" for the University of Notre Dame. ✶
36. Destiny
39. A _____ by any other name would smell as sweet.
40. What is said to Nanette
41. Although he was a Hoosier, Hoagy Carmichael's best known song might be "___ on My Mind." ✶
42. Bed and Breakfast (abbrev.)
44. Often paired with "moan"
48. Nip
49. Arthur Franklin Mapes wrote this official state poem. ✶
49. Will Shortz, the youngest-ever editor of the *New York Times'* crossword puzzle, majored in enigmatology (the study of puzzles) at which university? ✶
51. Earned Run Average
53. The first library of the Northwest territory was in this Indiana river city. ✶
56. To produce something, like an egg
57. Gene Stratton _____, Hoosier author, is most famous for *Freck-*

les and *The Girl of the Limberlost.* ✶
58. Chilly name of English painter who moved to Indiana and became famous for his paintings of Native Americans ✶
59. ___ Na Na
60. Strong scented herb beloved by felines

DOWN

1. Alantin
3. Education (abbrev.)
4. Female sheep
5. Indiana University is the only school in the United States that has been invited to perform a full opera at this prestigious New York Opera House. ✶
6. Ruth's mother-in-law
8. Most famous work of Indiana author Lew Wallace
9. Only ___ you
10. Van Denman Thompson was a professor of organ and composition at this Indiana college. ✶
11. A lutheran pastor from Evansville Walter Wangerin has written this book with the subtitle *The Bible as a Novel: The Book of* _____. ✶
13. Imagine trying to blow all of these out on your birthday! Meredith Nicholson's best known romantic mystery was called "*House of a Thousand* _____." ✶
16. The prize awarded in 1920 to Indiana writer Albert J. Beveridge for his book *John Marshall* ✶

18. Though better known for its football, this university is also home to the Snite Museum of Art. ✶
19. Tantrum
25. British slang for a toilet
28. *The Last Camel Died at* _____, is a novel by Elizabeth Peters
29. Spain's peninsula
30. A great American playwright, this Hoosier is most famous for his work *Fables in Slang.* ✶
31. Marriage vow: "I ___"
34. Droop
35. Catherine's honorary title
37. French word
38. _____, lose or draw

41. Kermit the Frog: "It's Not Easy Being _____"
43. Brother, to Uncle Remus
45. Gertrude Felton Harbart, born in Michigan City, Indiana, is known for her _____. ✶
46. The Chicago ____ was started by an Indiana dancer: Ruth Page. ✶
47. Teenagers' hangout
48. Black buck
50. Portal
51. Decree
52. Morning (abbrev.)
54. Do the ___
55. Grade-Point Average (abbrev.)

He was just... cool

When James Dean died in a car crash at age 24, he had appeared in a handful of films — only three where he was a major player: *Giant, Rebel Without a Cause* and *East of Eden*. However, he has left a legacy far larger than he probably would have ever believed or imagined.

Dean was born in Marion, Indiana, but spent the majority of his life in Fairmont, where he lived on his aunt and uncle's farm. It was going to high school in Fairmont that he discovered he had a flair for acting and began developing the skills that were to make him a star. He is now buried in Fairmont, where they celebrate his life with an annual James Dean Festival (including a look-alike contest) and a museum of family memoribilia that includes his grade-school artwork, his first motorcycle and the sweater that he had left at the dry cleaner before his death.

His family keeps up a terrific website if you are interested in learning more about the legend. Visit **www.jamesdean.com**.

Movies Made in Indiana

```
L E D J B X Y U P M L M B Z O E T U K Y
Y A D I L O H Y N N H O J Y S W R K E J
A P I P U T U O N E M T H G I E O T E S
W I R U E F B R I A N S S O N G H H R D
E E J S C O L V M C Q K C O Y O S E C N
H C K H H R P A Z I L Y O D O J L R S E
T E L E I C D U F J K S A S A L J Y S I
L O L D P I W X I A D L I W I J B A A R
L F D T S K X N C E A E B K I V F N R F
A E S O M E C A M E R U N N I N G W G R
G D N O R T T A S S U R U P Z A N H N U
N E M F O Y N A P M O C E H T N I I I O
I N Q A C L E E K B X R W R P A T T N F
O I Z R R L E U L J T A W R U K P E A G
G R V I P D F A Y C M I A Z G D I S M N
M G G O W B R E A K I N G A W A Y T T M
S A T A A U X L L M C M P S D K Y O S R
A N Y B T Q U F F E Q A S O M A C R E A
R E C A R G M O R F G N I L L A F Y B M
S Z N W O R I E H T F O E U G A E L A M
```

A Girl Named Sooner	*Four Friends*	*Rudy*
A League of Their Own	*Going All the Way*	*Some Came Running*
A Piece of Eden	*Hoosiers*	*Speedway*
Best Man in Grass Creek	*In the Company of Men*	*The Ryan White Story*
Blue Chips	*Johnny Holiday*	*To Please A Lady*
Breaking Away	*Madison*	*Viper*
Brian's Song	*Natural Born Killers*	*Winning*
Eight Men Out	*Prancer*	
Falling from Grace	*Pushed Too Far*	
	Rain Man	

Answer is on page 89

16

Hoosier Stars of TV and Film

Answer is on page 90

ACROSS

1. Indiana native JoAnne Worley was a regular on this '60s variety show. ★

6. Actress Marjorie Mann is famous for her performance as this character. ★

8. __ Sir, With Love

9. Hoosier James Best portrayed Sheriff Roscoe P. Coltrane on this popular television series. ★

12. Hometown of actor Forrest Tucker ★

14. Fort Wayne actress who became famous for her run on "Cheers." ★

15. Explosive

17. Birthplace of Indiana actress Florence Henderson. ★

18. Nickname for a Model T Ford: __ Lizzie

17

19. Indiana actor who played Samantha's husband, Darrin Stevens★

21. Gatsby's obsession

23. Traditional Christmas pudding

24. Soap opera that Indiana actor Robert Emhardt played MacKenzie Corey on★

27. Hoosier who replaced Barbara Walters on the "Today" show.★

28. What necessary item for the movie industry is manufactured in Warsaw, Indiana?★

29. Lincoln, to friends

30. Michael Warren appeared as Officer Bobby Hill on this 1980s cop drama.★

33. Dennis Quaid was a young man when he played a "cutter" in this movie about a bike race.★

36. Ms. Silverstone of Aerosmith video fame (no, she's not a hoosier)

38. __ at Joe's

39. Indiana University graduate Howard Ashman was the lyricist for *Beauty and the* _____.★

40. Hoosier Will Greer played "Grandpa" on this long-running series about a family in Virginia.★

DOWN

2. *Much __ About Nothing*

3. "I've ___ a Secret"

4. To show agreement

5. Japanese camera brand

6. Later a movie starring Tom Cruise, this TV series originally starred Hoosier Peter Lupus as Willy Armitage.★

7. This film, starring Cary Grant and Katharine Hepburn, was directed by Hoosier filmmaker Howard Hawks.★

8. Hoosier Florence Henderson is most famous for her role on this classic sitcom.★

10. Louisville pottery company

11. Born in 1931 in Marion, this actor personified rebellious youth.★

13. Hoosier Julia Barr appeared as Brooke English on this soap opera.★

16. Hoosier actor Steve McQueen's 1962 film *The ___ Lover*★

20. James Bond: *View to a* _____

22. Raid

25. Green tractor company: John _____

26. Sharing a last name with Superman's girlfriend, this actress from Macy, Indiana, first appeared in 1929's *Speakeasy*.★

27. Born in Lafayette, Indiana, this director has made seven movies with Robert Redford.★

31. This member of the Jackson family starred on "Diff'rent Strokes" and "Good Times" before becoming a pop star.★

32. A person's scruff

33. Most excellent

34. Simba's girlfriend

35. So be it

37. "I can't believe I ___ the whole thing."

Winners of the Indianapolis 500

```
V F F P D V M K D S O A I K K J D D C G
U S R E D U O S L C A N U W D R X T Q M
C N E T S K N R U T T M A N A Y R B U F
X E Y I J O L M U R P H Y W W O J R N N
O V E L T V M T S N S X N O S B O R F T
C A M L V I L L E N E U V E O C T Y O F
L W I O N C D S U L L I V A N S H S R J
I M O G N H R L K F O B M N U R O A N Z
W P S H O T E C A N Z R V D R A M N T K
A Q E C M U O L M P A T V R U E A U R I
L S V G H C U Y L H I H Q E T M S A K J
L E E O N N U K A N C T Y T H W L K Y G
A N N H S G E R P E S S T T E C O T D Q
R O O E Y U R I E D N T A I R H C O N Y
D J R E Y O B K D Y O R K K F E K L E F
A J T X U O G V L E S E C N O E H O Y T
R E S N U Y B B O B R B A Q R V A A U V
D N A L L O H E N T A O R W D E R P L V
T X C L A Z I E R Q P R B W Q R T E N F
B A T S E R A H A L L I H S I V A D M N
```

Al Unser	Cummings	Hill	Parsons	Souders
Al Unser Jr.	Davis	Holland	Petillo	Sullivan
Andretti	Dawson	Johncock	Rahal	Sweikert
Arnold	DePalma	Jones	Rathmann	Thomas
Bobby Unser	DePaolo	Keech	Resta	Villeneuve
Boyer	Donohue	Lazier	Roberts	Vukovich
Brack	Fittipaldi	Lockhart	Robson	Wallard
Bryan	Flaherty	Luyendyk	Rose	Ward
Castroneves	Foyt	Mears	Rutherford	Wilcox
Cheever	Frame	Meyer	Ruttman	
Chevrolet	Goux	Milton	Schneider	
Clark	Hanks	Montoya	Shaw	
Corum	Harroun	Murphy	Sneva	

Answer is on page 90

19

The Indianapolis Speedway

Answer is on page 91

ACROSS

1. Spanish for "yes"
2. NASCAR legend honored with an unofficial memorial at the Indianapolis Motor Speedway, Dale _____ ✫
7. 1986 Indy 500 winner: Bobby _____ ✫
10. British toilet
11. The Greatest ____ in Racing. ✫
13. First female Rookie of the Year: Lyn _____ ✫
15. Beam
16. Intravenous, in common parlance
17. Record-number of cars running at the finish of the Indy 500 race in 1911. ✫
20. Perfume
23. West African republic
25. Indefinite article used before

words starting with a vowel sound

26. The Indianapolis Speedway Hall __ Fame is located right at the track.✶

27. The winner of the 2000 Brickyard 400: Bobby ___✶

31. Race driver that drove in both the Indy 500 and the Charlotte 600 on the same day: John _____✶

32. Animated Film: ___ Age

33. Billy _____, the 1930 winner of the 500, was the first driver to average above 100 mph.✶

35. Before retiring from racing in 1982, Rick ____ had won eight 500-mile races.✶

37. The Company that sponsors the "Competitive Spirit" award to the lowest positioned car still running at the end of the race✶

39. Cloth border

43. Four-wheeled vehicles designed for passenger transportation

44. The first African-American driver in the Indianapolis 500: Willy T. ___.✶

45. 1998 Indy 500 winner that got to carry the Olympic Torch on a ceremonial lap around the Speedway✶

47. A four-time Indy 500 winner, __ Unser last won the race in 1987.✶

48. Computer graphic file

50. High, craggy hill

51. What the winner drinks after crossing the finish line✶

53. The _____ in Speed Award is

presented by the Raybestos brakes corporation.✶

55. The Indianapolis 500 race is 200 ____ around the track.✶

57. Carburetion Day features the popular Indy ___ Stop Challenge, where the race teams get to show their stuff.✶

58. "Ladies and gentlemen, start your _____"✶

63. Blue _____

64. Woo

65. In 1996, Arie _____ was the first driver to break the 235-mph barrier in a practice lap.✶

DOWN

1. Ergo

3. Three-time Indy 500 winner and 1997 Pace Car driver: Johnny _____.✶

4. People love to tour Gasoline ___ as part of their Indianapolis Speedway experience.✶

5. A kind of deer

6. I ___

7. The youngest winner of the 500, at the age of 22, was Tony ____ in 1952.✶

8. Ogle

9. Ready, set, ___!

11. Number of cars to finish in 1966, the year the fewest number of cars finished the race✶

12. Consumes

14. Palm

18. Nine Indy winners were lucky with this car number.✶

19. 1985 Indy 500 winner Danny _____✶

21. 2000 IRL National Champion,

Tony_____ ★
22. Knock out (abbrev.)
24. Winner of the first NASCAR race at the Brickyard: Jeff _____ ★
25. Jason's ship
28. Although most have been covered up with asphalt, the original ____ that paved the speedway are still visible at the start/finish line. ★
29. 1996 Indy 500 winner: _____ Lazier. ★
30. This film star and believer in reincarnation was on hand to kiss the winner of the 1958 race: Shirley _____. ★
34. "Back Home Again in ____" is sung before every Indy 500. ★
36. Quiet!
38. "The wheels on the __ go round and round."
40. ____ Fittilpaldi won the Indy 500 in 1989 and 1993. ★
41. The symbol of Scott Goodyear's homeland: the ____ leaf. ★

42. Team Green driver that felt he was the winner of the controversial 2002 Indianapolis 500: Paul ____. ★
43. Aids and ____
45. Reach
46. Moose's cousin
48. Insured for more than $150,000, this award for winning the 500 carries bas-relief portraits of all Indy 500 winners. ★
49. Four-time Indy winner: A.J.____ ★
52. In 1999, this late-night television host had the honor of driving the Indy Pace Car: Jay____. ★
54. Get
55. Hawaiian party
56. Getting to start first is called "winning the ____." ★
58. Go get'__, tiger!
59. "__ tell it on the Mountain"
60. Abbreviation for Indiana ★
61. Public transport in Chicago
62. You're __ far away

Racing Fatalities

There have been 66 deaths at the Indianapolis Speedway: 39 drivers, 14 mechanics, four racing personnel, eight spectators and one that is deemed to be a "miscellaneous" death. What does that mean? In 1931, young Wilbur Brink was killed by the Indianapolis 500 without even being at the race. The 11-year old was playing in his yard when a wheel from the car of Billy Arnold flew out of the Speedway and across Georgetown Road and struck him.

Indiana Sports Teams

```
E Z P T Q Y K C S R E T S E R O F N O T G N I T N U H F K D
T X U X P D L I N D I A N A P O L I S I N D I A N S L K J W
I H T N L M E V A N S V I L L E O T T E R S Q N E V J D B Z
E P N R F O N F J O S R E D A S U R C O S I A R A P L A V W
W Y V P   I O T W Z V Q T P Z N O F Q K B A K     S B A P
K U S O   V L P Y X C T M R S V K H F O O Q L     L E L K
S W L K   P I I B I J W Q O A X B W R C K Q U     I V P B
R E F F   S D R I B E R I F A N A I D N I T H     N A N M
W G A L   Q M A A B A D C F N Y X S W N D N F     D N O B
C I C Q   C E Z R E P K X G L Z Z N B O J X K     I S T I
R N E X   F O R T W A Y N E W I Z A R D S V B     A V R N
I D I G   P U R D U E B O I L E R M A K E R S     N I E D
C I A M   H U Z J A C X E V S C W S D V M Z D     A L D I
H A M N   G M F O R T W A Y N E K O M E T S K     S L A A
M N N S   G T U W J C J V U Q Z O A S B J Y T     T E M N
O A U D                                           A P E A
N H N N                                           T U F P
D O O E J K L T U S C F A I     I N D I A N A F E V E R I O
R O P G P F O X G R E W W T     R N R Q Y J V Z O B S P G L
O S R E C A P A N A I D N I     R B X J H S C H E E Y L H I
O I F L F M A O A N I H G C     A U W G Q S G F Y I C E T S
S E D A T X U A I K S G H V     M K P Z U F Q L E O A A I C
T R W N D F V J C P O B L S     Q P O V H K G S V G M C N O
E S G A M S U L Y S E L M J     H Q Z J H Y N G Q R O E G L
R Y R I Z T F X S L N Q I N     D E P A U W T I G E R S I T
S G O D L L U B R E L T U B     K B E Z H Z Q Y I D E H R S
X E D N S S M T M D Y M R I     I N D I A N A B L A S T I N
Q I Z I N X F E I V F M V Q     O N I K M B E O X K F Y S K
Q F P M G R D A S K W A H R E V L I S D N E B H T U O S H S
K P E D U B O I S C O U N T Y D R A G O N S H I Y N E D N N
```

Butler Bulldogs	Huntington Foresters	Indianapolis Indians
Depauw Tigers	Indiana Blast	Notre Dame Fighting Irish
Dubois County Dragons	Indiana Fever	Purdue Boilermakers
Evansville Otters	Indiana Firebirds	Richmond Roosters
Evansville Purple Aces	Indiana Hoosiers	South Bend Silverhawks
Fort Wayne Komets	Indiana Legends	Valparaiso Crusaders
Fort Wayne Wizards	Indiana Pacers	
	Indiana State Sycamores	
	Indianapolis Colts	

Answer is on page 91

Indiana Sports

Answer is on page 92

ACROSS

2. Home of the Indianapolis Indians: _____ Field ★
6. American automaker
8. Gear
9. Youngest March sister
11. Indiana basketball legend from French Lick: Larry _____ ★
12. Radium (Periodic Table)
13. Procession
14. Showstopper from *A Chorus Line*
16. German father
17. Affirmative
18. Be aware of
19. Carte
21. Bow
22. Awarded to the winner of the Indiana-Purdue football game every year ★
23. Bashful
24. Taboo
26. Awarded to the winner of the Purdue-Notre Dame football game every year: The _____ ★

28. March
29. Nickname for Indiana University teams★
33. Permute
34. Chuck Taylor of Columbus, Indiana, is the founder of what tennis shoe company?★
37. Nickname of University of Evansville's sports teams★
38. Beck
41. Cove
42. German physicist, George Simon ____
43. At no time
44. In what sport does IU hold 20 consecutive Big Ten titles?★
46. Black
47. Director ____ Lee
49. Jim Rayl, Kokomo-born basketball star, is better known by his nickname "The Splendid ____."★
53. Warble
54. Elvis Presley pooch
55. Cause and ____

DOWN

1. Legendary Indiana swimming and diving coach: "Doc" _____★
3. City that hosts the RCA Tennis Championships★
4. Auto
5. "Stand ____ Me"
6. Original home of the Detroit Pistons★
7. First lady of disco: ____ Summer
10. This Purdue player caught Joe DiMaggio's last out.★
11. Nickname for Purdue University teams★
15. Home of the Indiana Basketball Hall of Fame★
19. Basketball coach for both Ball State and Indiana University: Branch ____★
20. Cupid's love
25. Second player to record more than 1000 points, 700 rebounds and 100 steals at Indiana State: Jim ____★
27. Pitcher who attended Indiana State University: Tommy ____★
28. Notre Dame's first paid football coach: Frank ____★
30. This Hoosier was the first player to pitch a perfect game during the World Series.★
31. John Lujack, John Lattner and Paul Hornung were two-sport stars at Notre Dame and winners of the ____ Trophy.★
32. Known as "Baby Bull," this athlete dropped out of school two years early to join the Indiana Pacers for the 1971-72 season.★
33. Home of the Indiana Football Hall of Fame ★
35. Guilty mind, latin: Mens ____.
36. Morning moisture
39. Twin
40. Adam's mate
41. Grain covering
44. Window frame
45. Clinton's Vice-President
47. Agriculture (abbrev.)
48. __, fight, win!
50. Purchase Order (abbrev.)
51. Tai ethnic group in China.
52. Go __ and out the window.

Permanent Residents of Indiana

Answer is on page 92

ACROSS

1. Behold
2. L.A. _____
5. First three-time winner of the Indianpolis 500 and co-developer of the Meyer-Drake engine: Louis _____ ★
8. Bachelor of Science
9. Novelist and playwright from Indiana, _____ Tarkington rests in Crown Hill cemetary in Indianapolis. ★
11. Author and playwright George ___ is buried in Kentland, IN. ★
15. First name of entrepreneur and department store owner L.S. Ayres ★
16. Important to a pitcher
18. _____ Carmichael, the songwriter who gave the world "Pennies from Heaven," is buried in Bloomington. ★
19. This sad clown is buried in Lafayette: Emmett _____. ★
21. Suitable
23. Environmental Protection Agency
24. Image
25. Daniel's younger brother,

26

Squire _____, is buried in the Cavern's that bear is name in southern Indiana.★

26. Warner Brothers
28. Common rodent
29. Actor McKellen
30. Dream state
31. Coach famous for saying "Win one for the Gipper" is buried in South Bend.★
32. Indiana politician whose name sounds like a word that means "finished," Williamson _____ donated the land that Hanover College now sits on and rests permanently nearby.★
33. Roseanne's movie, ___-*Devil*
34. The 23rd President of the United States, Benjamin _____, returned to Indianpolis for his final resting place.★
35. The father of entomology, Thomas Say, was the first to seriously study _____. His book, *American Entomology,* is considered a classic.★
37. James Baskett, the actor who portrayed Uncle _____ in Disney's *Song of the South*, is buried in Indianapolis.★
41. Overtime
43. Infamous gangster who is buried in Crown Hill cemetary in Indianapolis: John _____.★
45. "Beware the Ides of _____"
46. Island country with American bases
47. A renowned educator and Indiana University president and chancellor, Herman B. ___ rests in Bloomington near the uni-

versity he served for eight decades.★
48. _____ & Bradstreet
49. Supreme Court Justice Sherman _____ is buried in New Albany.★

DOWN

1. Pharmaceutical giant Eli _____ rests at Crown Hill cemetary in Indianapolis.★
2. Crazy as a _____
3. Preposition
4. Young Cicero resident and AIDS activist who fought for his right to continue his education: Ryan _____.★
6. Another word for serf
7. Bombyx
8. Exist
9. Emeril's catchphrase
10. Most famous for writing ____ *of the Limberlost,* Indiana author Gene Stratton-Porter has a memorial in Rome City.★
12. This rebel without a cause is buried in his hometown of Fairmount: James _____.★
13. St. Louis baseball legend Mordecai Brown, affectionately known as "_____ Finger," is buried in Terre Haute.★
14. WWII Journalist that the Indiana University School of Journalism is named for, Ernie ____, has a memorial in Dana.★
17. These outlaw brothers who share a name with a gambling resort in Nevada, were the first train robbers. They were hanged by vigilantes.★

20. Abraham's mother, Nancy Hanks _____, died when he was nine years old and is buried in Spencer County.★

21. Actress from the golden age of Hollywood, Frances _____, is buried in Indianapolis.★

22. John B. Crafton, a wealthy quarry owner who is buried in Bloomington, died in the sinking of this mammoth ship.★

23. Although his final resting place is in North Carolina, it was only fitting that this racing legend have a memorial in Indiana.★

25. Permanent Crawfordsville resident Lew Wallace, former minister to Turkey and a Union general, might be most famous for this book:_____★

26. ___, lose or draw

27. Sharing a last name with the family who hires Mary Poppins, Henry _____ was a race car driver and USAC official.★

32. Terre Haute socialist who ran for president five times: Eugene V. _____★

36. Cole _____, musical great known for such songs as "You're the Top" and "Miss Otis Regrets," is buried in Peru, Indiana.★

38. An original sponsor of the Indianapolis 500, ____ Engineering was owned by brothers Charles and Fred.★

39. Credited with saving the Indianapolis Motor Speedway Anton _____.★

40. Shannon Hoon, lead singer for the band _____ Melon, died tragically of a drug overdose before he was 30 and is buried in Dayton, Indiana.★

42. Legendary Indiana basketball star whose son and grandson also went on to basketball fame: Paul _____.★

44. Grace Kelly movie: *High*____

45. Grinder

INDIANA
PLACES
Our Geography

A Rich and Varied State

From the rolling hills of the Ohio Valley to the Northern Indiana cornfields that extend as far as the eye can see and from the largest inland shipyard to the golden dome at Notre Dame, the state of Indiana is rich in beauty, diverse of feature and unique in the destinations it has to offer any traveler.

The following puzzles will test your knowledge of the many attractions of Indiana. I have included some of the most interesting destinations in the state in these puzzles, and you will need to know in which town or city they are located in order to fill in the crossword.

I hope you learn enough from these puzzles to consider discovering some of these wonderful spots for yourself — I know it made me want to hit the road and see more of the state for myself.

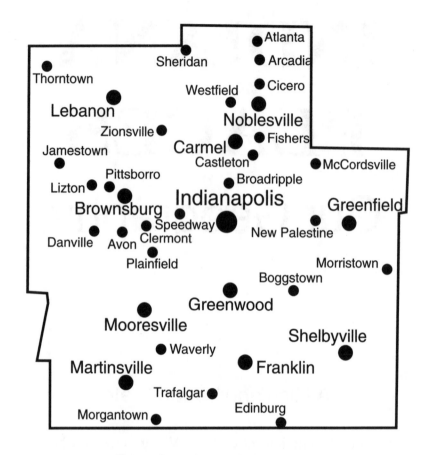

Starting in the Middle

Central Indiana has many attractions that center around Indianapolis, our state capital and largest city. Professional sports, world-class museums, great restaurants, live theater and dance can all be found in the "Circle City." Indianapolis is also now home to the NCAA headquarters and their museum, the Hall of Champions.

Also close to the heart of most Hoosiers, the Indiana High School Athletic Association is headquartered in Indianapolis. If you've seen the movie *Hoosiers* or ever been fortunate enough to attend a high school basketball sectional game, you'll know how seriously we take our youth sports.

Indianapolis Attractions

```
L I X H C I N E D O M E T H E A T E R Y O
T P N C O N S E C O F I E L D H O U S E J
M O A D I D K Z Z T I N J C G V L W X I K
H O Y A I I K Z T Q S G Z X R S X F R F F
C Z R E G A L L I V E L P P I R D A O R B
M S E R H N N A G F R E M T Q I D M U I F
L I N D I A N A W A R M E M O R I A L A A
G L I T M S R N S V V I V H Y Z K S P V K
K O W L A T B A R T S G A R D E N U S U I
Z P Y F X A Z U V R A C E W A Y P A R K M
S A E N T T T Y T X F T A L P E C Y J X X
R N L T H E C H I L D R E N S M U S E U M
Z A S Q E M M Y S T E R Y C A F E R K H I
O I A Z A U T G N Z F R W F A E I C Q H J
J D E Q T S Z S O D M Q H K V P V D J O U
T N L Y E E L L A H S E W O L C I I U O B
O I J O R U A W A G U N C E U U M T A G K
M U E S U M G R O J L E T I E S J Z O N U
E X W H I T E R I V E R G A R D E N S L L
J Q R E R A U Q S N I A T N U O F A F O Z
Z R C W G H O S I K B Q D W S A B H L B H
```

Artsgarden	Fountain Square	Mystery Cafe
Broad Ripple Village	IMAX Theater	Raceway Park
CineDome Theater	Indiana State Capitol	The Childrens
Clowes Hall	Indiana State Museum	Museum
Conseco Fieldhouse	Indiana War Memorial	White River Gardens
Easley Winery	Indianapolis Zoo	
Eiteljorg Museum	Morris Butler House	

Answer is on page 93

Central Indiana Wonders

Answer is on page 93

ACROSS

1. Swanky
3. Riley Home Complex ★
7. Harry's friend Hedwig
10. Also
11. Robbie Burns' slang for "Endure"
13. Grover Museum ★
14. Indefinite article used before words starting with vowel sounds
15. Lead singer for U2
16. Home to the Indianapolis Ice ★
19. Hitchcock: *To __ a Thief*
21. The guilty party in *The Fugitive* was missing one of these.
23. Moral depravity
24. Running direction (goes with fro)
25. Indianapolis sports team that plays in the RCA Dome ★
28. Home to the Indianapolis Indians ★

30. Patti Smythe's 1980s band
31. Cut lengthwise
33. Tiny pool
34. The Museum of Miniature Houses ✮
37. Showoff or a sandwich meat
38. Tombstone salutation
40. Chateau Thomas Winery ✮
43. Negative or a hornless sheep
44. Indiana, to the postmaster ✮
45. Indianapolis concert and broadway musical theater venue ✮
48. Iron, on the periodic table
49. Information, if you're in a hurry
51. When used with the adjective "old," this was a nickname for the devil.
53. Baseball home run hitter
55. An expression of sorrow
57. Music group that sang "You Shook Me All Night Long"
58. Humorous satire
59. Indianapolis Motor Speedway✮
60. Honeymaker

DOWN

1. Home to the Indiana Pacers, Indiana Fever and Indianapolis Firebirds ✮
2. Santa laugh
4. Racing family
5. Verizon Wireless Music Center ✮
6. Deliver us from ____
7. Either's partner

8. Astrange
9. Late night talk show host NOT from Indiana
11. To remove an orange's stem
12. Native American tribe from Oregon
17. Solid water
18. Mickey and kind
20. Preferred soda temperature in the United States
22. Kanga's child
25. Alder grove in Britain
26. Slangish "goodbye"
27. Cunning
29. Colonel Eli Lilly Civil War Museum and NCAA Hall of Champions are located here ✮
32. Opposite of Eros: Death instinct
33. Afternoon
34. Indianapolis Raceway Park ✮
35. Bert's roommate
36. King of the jungle
39. Post-injury treatment (abbrev.)
41. Not a single one
42. Stonehenge fan
46. Opposite of "that"
47. Something real men don't eat — according to a popular 1980s book.
48. Fated to die (in Scotland)
50. Name for back of your neck
52. One who refuses to join a union
54. You're relaxed if you can describe yourself as content to rest on these.
56. The one Adam blamed for it all

Indiana High School Nicknames

Answer is on page 94

ACROSS

1. On the Bridge __ Avignon
2. To tell all one knows
10. Russell Crowe didn't attend Hammond Gavit, but he could be their mascot. ★
12. Hard to believe, but these slippery creatures are the mascots for both Clay City and Eminence. ★
13. Gypsy
16. Wabash High School has this Native American tribe as their team nickname. ★
18. Not well
19. ___ 'M' for Murder
21. "Oh, say, can you ____..."
22. Jimtown's nickname is one that sounds like a breaking and entering term. ★
24. Not us
25. Indianapolis Northwest has this original synonym for astronauts as their nickname. ★

26. Laugh
28. Travels in a swarm
29. Adolescent
30. Northfield's mascots are the _____ men. ★
31. Five high schools in Indiana share this demonic nickname.★
33. _____: the town that calls its teams "Rox." ★
34. Period
36. Madison-Grant shares its nickname with socks. ★
38. This town shares its name with a make-up company
39. Anger
40. Penn High's mascot can be guessed with this clue: Who couldn't put Humpty Dumpty together again?★
41. To exist
42. We're sure that Oregon-Davis didn't adapt this nickname because of comic Goldthwait. ★
43. Linton-Stockton's nickname stems from the large number of coal mines found in its part of the state. ★
45. Ben Davis, one of the largest high schools in the state, also has the biggest mascot. ★
47. Rising Sun's nickname can also mean multiple black eyes. ★
48. Depression

DOWN

1. It won't take you 101 nights to guess Pendleton Heights nickname. ★
3. Abbrev. for agriculture
4. Tipton shares its nickname with Duke University. ★
5. Opposite of subtract
6. Grab
7. Nick and ___ Charles
8. You'll be dazzled with the bright nickname of Franklin Central. ★
9. Garrett, Indiana, must have lots of train tracks through town to justify this nickname. ★
11. Twinkle, twinkle: the nickname for both Bedford North Lawrence and Western Boone★
14. Despite the nickname, we are confident that Pekin's high school uses more than three players on each of their teams.★
15. Vincennes-Lincoln's sports teams are known by this "wonder"-ful nickname.★
17. Washington High School chose the tool that chopped down the cherry tree as its nickname. ★
20. Race car driver, ___ Foyt
23. These night-time bandits are the nickname for Mt. Vernon's sports teams. ★
27. 18 schools in Indiana have this cat-like nickname, making it the most popular in this state. ★
28. Perhaps Hobart's nickname comes from an abundance of masons in its town. ★
30. Steve Alford's high school: ___ Castle.★
31. Blushing
32. Although it isn't a mighty nickname, it makes sense for Logansport. ★
34. These mythical creatures are the

mascorts for Argos, New Palestine and Silver Creek.★

35. Also
37. The only school to have their nickname start with a "z" is Rochester.★
40. Sacramento and Cass High School share this nickname.★

41. Not just one of us
43. Not you
44. Attica's nickname is the ___ Ramblers.★
45. General Electric
46. What ___ Love?

Indy's Race
by Sally Morge Hassler

"Gentlemen, start your engines"
Is how the race begins.
But the big question, my friend,
Is how will the race end?
Since 1911, they've come to the track,
Come next May, I'm sure they'll be back.
Owners and drivers, pit crews and fans,
Lining Gasoline Alley and filling the stands.
Brimming with wonder, power and pride,
Ready to view the spectacular ride.
Two hundred laps around the track,
Five hundred miles in a racing pack.
When the cars begin, there are thirty-three.
When the race is over, how many will there be?
The Indy 500, the famed speedway,
Still home of the greatest races today!

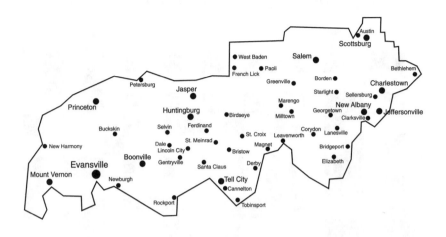

Southern Indiana

Southern Indiana is home to the world's second-largest clock, the largest inland boat manufacturer, the Falls of the Ohio, Squire Boone Caverns and the historic and beautiful French Lick resort.

Did you know that the man whom many consider to be the greatest president in the history of our nation, Abraham Lincoln, lived in Southern Indiana from 1816 to 1830? His formative years, from age seven to age 21, were spent in what is now named Lincoln City, Indiana. The National Parks Service operates the Lincoln Boyhood National Memorial, where you can visit the Lincoln Memorial Visitor Center, walk the Lincoln Boyhood Trail or see the Lincoln Historical Farm. Nearby, the Lincoln Amphitheatre hosts continual showings of "Young Abe Lincoln," a musical outdoor drama about the years Abraham Lincoln spent in Indiana. The play promises to show: "Through the deaths of his mother and sister and his first brush with slavery, you'll see how Abraham's youth in Indiana helped make him one of our nation's greatest presidents."

Sightseeing in Southern Indiana

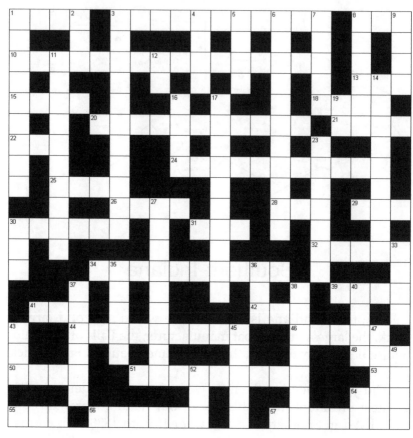

Answer is on page 94

ACROSS

1. Lamech's father
3. Falls of the Ohio State Park ✭
8. Dracula rodent
10. West Baden Springs National Historic Landmark ✭
13. College admission test
15. Stop, ___ and listen
18. Sicily mount
20. Colonel William Jones State Historic Site ✭
21. The weather kind, not the Carly Simon kind
22. *Oh Brother Where ___ Thou?*
24. Holiday World & Splashing Safari ✭
25. Wooden trainmaker
26. Dragnet actor
28. Golf ball holder
29. Elementary school parent organization
30. Deam Lake State Park ✭

31. Type of evergreen
32. Mary Tyler Moore spinoff: Lou ____
34. Indiana Railway Museum, French Lick Springs Resort & Spa ✷
39. Verb used to describe the act of hitting someone over the head with an umbrella
41. Mineral spring resorted to for cures
42. Scout's neighbor: ____ Radley
44. Huber Orchard & Winery and The Forest Discovery Center ✷
46. Southern Indiana is known as "Indiana's _____ County."✷
48. To snatch quickly
50. Dr. Ted's Musical Marvels ✷
51. Monastery Immaculate Conception ✷
53. Life span in Latin
54. Animal kept for pleasure rather than utility
55. One if by land, two if by ____
56. What the settlement of New Harmony, Indiana, was intended to be ✷
57. Sycamore Springs Park ✷

DOWN

1. Carnegie Center for Art & History and the Culbertson Mansion State Historic Site ✷
2. *Some Like it* ____
3. Charlestown State Park ✷
4. Hershey's famous chocolate bites
5. Alter
6. Lincoln Boyhood National Memorial and the Lincoln State Park ✷
7. Elmer's wife
8. Snack for a monkey
9. Practicing diplomacy
11. Pigeon Roost State Historic Site and Hardy Lake ✷
12. Chicago's subway
14. Blue Heron House Vineyard & Winery ✷
16. Greek god of love
17. Angel Mounds State Historic Site and the Reitz Home Museum, Willard Library ✷
19. NBC: Must-See ____
23. Marengo Cave National Landmark ✷
27. Warrick County Museum and Scales Lake Park ✷
30. Honeymaker
33. *Bewitched*: Samantha's husband's boss
35. *Three's Company* hangout: The ____ Beagle
36. Material used for Frosty's pipe
37. Dubois County Museum and the Indiana Baseball Hall of Fame ✷
38. Squire Boone Caverns ✷
40. Imagine
43. Finis
45. Zoan
47. Excessively favorable reviews
49. Roman empire spa town
52. Genetic blueprint
54. Circle geometry term

Southern Indiana Counties

```
M A S L R F V L N E C S G N I N N E J G
M H Z F Y S L U A O J S Q W G R E E N E
D U B S S T W M V O S E D Y O L F V Q N
Z M M A K I E B I G V I R B K F P N O F
I Z Y K E K O Y L M W V R A E H E E K F
N Y O L J O W B L D N A L R E Z T I W S
A L E S K B W D U O E D S T A Z L E P S
K P N A V A Y R S D L O T H A H M C S G
K G S O Q K U N I O N E W O I H O V B P
B I A U L S H E L B Y N I L K N A R F I
H C X Q H O H W J A C K S O N N G U N K
X X B N J U D S F M E R W M D Y H T R E
H Q E P J H Y S Y T E O A E Q A A A O G
J B X Y R R E P E C N E R W A L L C W N
X B X T E M S F N W L B R N F C X E F A
J C D O S L O E O O U V I G O O W D U R
S K U B C U P R J R H T C E J M R Q W O
R G F N O S B I G S R X K N O X G D R A
J A H R T L X H R A R N O N Y S O T Z V
M U K D T L P P M H N N S X L W X M O N
```

Bartholomew	Franklin	Monroe	Shelby
Brown	Gibson	Morgan	Spencer
Clark	Greene	Ohio	Sullivan
Clay	Harrison	Orange	Switzerland
Crawford	Jackson	Owen	Union
Daviess	Jefferson	Perry	Vanderburgh
Dearborn	Jennings	Pike	Vigo
Decatur	Johnson	Posey	Warrick
Dubois	Knox	Ripley	Washington
Fayette	Lawrence	Rush	
Floyd	Martin	Scott	

Answer is on page 95

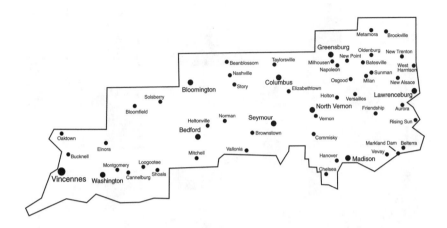

South Central Indiana

Looking for an outdoor adventure? Why not visit the Hoosier National Forest west of Bedford or the Amish communities in Daviess County? Also in the south-central part of Indiana is Monroe Reservoir, if boating or fishing are more in your line, and don't forget the equestrian facilities at the Brown County State Park for those of you who enjoy horseback riding.

For those of you looking for more "urban activities," South Central Indiana also boasts riverboat casinos in Lawrenceburg, Rising Sun and Belterra. You can play the slots, hit the golf course, catch a Las Vegas-style show or relax in an elegant spa— all within this one region!

Indiana University is also located here in the beautiful rolling hills, and at the school where DNA was discovered and the music school is continually in the top five in the nation, intellectual and musical events are always available for your enjoyment. Oh, and they have a pretty good basketball team too.

South Central Indiana Highlights

Answer is on page 95

ACROSS

1. Fancy word for beige
5. Weberding's Carving Shop and the Raspberry Festival in July ✯
10. Manual rowing tool
11. Opposite of yes
12. Powerpuff Girls' adversary
14. Indiana's Daviess County is ____ Country ✯
15. Either's partner
16. English professors' conference (abbrev.)
17. Muscatatuck Park ✯
21. What __ love?
22. Cherokee Ridge Gardens, the Monroe County Historical Society, Oliver Winery, and Monroe Lake ✯
25. Between eight and 10
26. Goes with Sesame (abbrev.)
27. Antique Auto and Race Car Museum and Bluespring Caverns Park ✯
30. National Muzzle Loading Rifle Association ✯

31. Annum
32. Don't get mad; get _____
35. Baseball pitcher's stat
36. Grand Victoria Casino & Resort and the Navy Bean Fall Festival ✷
38. Flying art form
40. Spring Mill State Park ✷
43. Museum celebrating the 1954 Indiana high school basketball state champions ✷
44. Starve Hollow State Recreation Area ✷
46. Upper body
50. President of the Confederacy
51. Whitewater Canal State Historic Site ✷
55. Hitchcock thriller: _ *Window*
59. Wind
60. Setting of many Kipling tales
61. The Hillforest Mansion and the Victorian Christmas celebration ✷
62. Bar trivia game
63. Lucy's neighbors: Ethel and _____
64. Bert's twin
65. Nickname of Lawrence County ✷

DOWN

2. Steam Cliff Herb Farm and Tea Room ✷
3. Recommended way to travel through Europe
4. Star name for bear
6. Shakespearian "soon"
7. Bullfight cheer
8. Perfect North Ski Slopes and the Argosy Casino and Hotel ✷
9. So be it
13. Shakamak State Park ✷
18. Home away from home

19. Person who elects officials
20. Graham Farms Cheese Factory ✷
23. To classify is to bring _____
24. British islands
25. Chateau Thomas Winery Tasting Room, the T.C. Steele Historic Site and the Brown County State Park ✷
28. The white-tailed variety of this animal is found in many Indiana forests.
29. *Titanic* love song, "Near, ___, wherever you are...."
33. George Rogers Clark National Historical Park and the Indiana Military Museum ✷
34. Number of muses
37. Jamie Lee Curtis book, *Today, I Feel* _____
39. Unusual farm building found in Brownstown, Indiana ✷
41. Bakersfield Raceway Park ✷
42. Lanier Mansion, the Jefferson County Historical Society Museum and Clifty Falls State Park ✷
45. Retirement savings
47. Gold (in Spain)
48. Agatha Christie's mystery train
49. Architecture for crossing a river
52. Mystery masked man's sidekick
53. Substitute (abbrev.)
54. Adam was supposedly the first
56. Not the beginning or the middle but the ___
57. Slang term for time or space purchased to promote a product
58. First two letter's in Tigger's "TTFN" stand for these two syllables
63. Not your friend

State Historic Sites

```
V P M V E L F J T E U I I L O O R A U C D W G H V Z X R O E
Y L Q W L S H E O R Y A A Z C B U D X T U I N M J P N L J W
D J I P S K K I C A G U C D V J F I R Q P L X R O O E J B G
C P H M L Y A S R A V E Z H F T E A C F M L Y F W B Z M F O
K Z Z I B R R V N C L L B Q X C Y M J U J N G E P J N R G E
M V D O P E U U G E Q P Z X O A I Y F U O G C S B Z G Z E Z
E P Y N R U R C Z S M H H T B I K E B Y J G Y R I D H K N M
O V U M D P Z L S F R L R T W G B M T G N E Z G K C O Q K R
D V F Z C J N C O P E L Q H R T S O O R N O E G I P A W E M
P X N A J A O H J S A L C I E I Y H C W B R M Z N A D Q V I
E P K N W W G A T B T M S M K B B S S L H G M R T N L R T I
E L C O X W J V O K C S O W H I T E W A T E R C A N A L A S
K R J I B Q S K O A O H T E U D K N L A N R U M P H V C Q M
M Z D S V I Y B V M E M Z A X A C O Z Y N O E U S N W M U O
K N Q N N M W E A L C L D W T J S J F X P G N Q S D K E P G
W D M A N S F I E L D R O L L E R M I L L E E H B S S Q N B
T E U M V R R E A W B H T E C S H A L P X R I L I U D T G B
K U L N S M T T F R V Q F Q L U D I W A C S C N M E U W H P
O R V O U S W H R S U W K R H O M L S Z A C I E R O F Q T Z
L G M S C V O P E U D E X B E H K L V T D L T L Y E U D U P
F E E T G F A F X J U X G O W N W I X F O A I E B A I N W Q
W U Q R J W X C T F H K G V O I Q W R C T R U V I Y F G D L
M J S E J V G N W E O Z O D S F T L M S D K I Z A I J Q H S
Q B E B C A G L C Z O Y Y I M F U E A G J P H C G W Z B D C
R H F L F O Z E M O H R E T R O P N O T T A R T S E N E G P
B O Q U Z B J W H K O B P G E C A O D H Y R G N V I D V U Y
P J E C R D H B U C K K C J E I F L O U Q K O U D W T U J V
Q E N D S W G Z U C V U O M D V M O B Q A Z S T V B L E A G
U P S H S M I W A O L B H N Q E U C B K Z Y Y T T T V B D B
J V S N O I S N A M R E I N A L D A V X Y W B I W U S B Z W
```

Angel Mounds
Colonel William Jones Home
Corydon
Culbertson Mansion
Ernie Pyle Birthplace
Gene Stratton Porter Home
George Rogers Clark Park
Grissom Air Museum
Indiana State Museum

Lanier Mansion
Levi Coffin House
Limberlost State Historic Site
Mansfield Roller Mill
New Harmony
Pigeon Roost
TC Steele Home
Whitewater Canal

Answer is on page 96

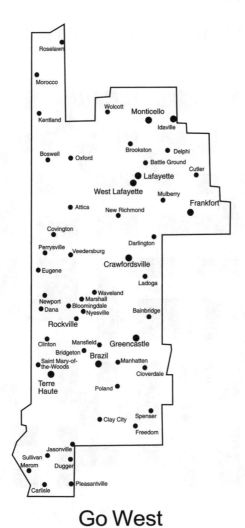

Go West

Along the Illinois border, you'll find the birthplace of the great World War II journalist Ernie Pyle, covered bridges, beautifully crafted pottery, the Indiana Beach amusement park and Purdue University.

Mushrooms, pumpkins, strawberries, herbs, guourds, maple syrup are all celebrated in local festivals and are available in abundant fresh quantities at street-side stands and markets.

So, hungry for fun or for delicious fresh food? Go west!

Western Indiana Attractions

Answer is on page 96

ACROSS

1. Ben-Hur Museum, Lane Place Antebellum Museum, Old Jail Museum and Wabash College are here ★
6. Speed word — or a brand of razor
11. Repeat this syllable three times and it's a dance.
12. Home to the Indiana Wolf Park★
15. Wabash and Erie canals★
17. Paul Revere, to name one
19. Exist
20. Zero, none, zilch
23. Santa's main word in conversation
25. Wayans' brothers: __ *Money*
26. Bacon's partner
27. Word describing one who hates all that is foreign
28. Indiana Beach slogan: "There's more than ____ in Indiana."★

46

29. Purdue University ★
32. It sounds like a tart thief, but this spelling actually refers to part of a church.
34. America's largest public coral reef display is in this Indiana city. ★
36. Lay about in a relaxed fashion
37. Take advantage of opportunities offered
39. Tippecanoe Battlefield ★
42. Who? ___?
43. Turkey Run State Park ★
45. Letters that come before the anticipated end of a trip
46. County known for its 32 covered bridges ★
48. *Grease*: "Look at me, I'm Sandra ___."
49. James Bond: __ Russia with Love
51. Stephen King book
52. Do, re, ___, fa ...
54. Ernie Pyle State Historic Site ★
55. Shakespeare had one in midsummer; Bugs Bunny has one about a light brown hare
58. Indianapolis 500: _____ lane
60. Jack and Jill's traveling case
61. Opening night destination (European spelling)
62. Proportion

DOWN

1. Terre Haute Brewing Co.'s famous name beer★
2. Something inspired by a muse
3. Payment charged for a service
4. Entryway
5. "She __ him around by his nose."
7. Throbbing pain

8. 22nd letter of the Greek alphabet
9. Expression of laughter on paper
10. Everything
13. Entice
14. German never
16. A bump on the end of something
18. Mineral word
21. To express oneself briefly is to be _____.
22. Billie Creek Village and Inn ★
23. Another word for rabbit
24. Broadway show: *My Pal* ___
25. Indiana Beach Amusement Resort and Lake Shafer ★
30. Something that can be scared out of one
31. Apprehension
33. Word for state of not being well
35. Adjective used to describe wandering knights
37. To put something right
38. Abbreviated name for the definitive reference book that lists all active publishers
40. Glass made by blending two or more colored glasses
41. 1954 sci-fi classic
44. Robinson House Galleries ★
46. Captain Hook, for one
47. New Jersey hangout
48. Bette and Jefferson
50. Canoe paddle
53. Elephant poacher's trophy
56. Not edible by vegetarians
57. Something one needs to be helped out of
59. Grain necessary to the Quaker company

Indiana State Parks

```
W D O W H S P R I N G M I L L Q O C I N
X H M N B Y T N U O C N W O R B Z N V I
F T I I P T O C L S D U L J V R L H X P
N F I T B D U Y J I M E W S M O C R T J
U L D P E M A E A R S H I D C J Y O N T
R S F M P W B N B R S U T N C Z H V J R
Y E A U S E A A C A M U I U O V P L M S
E E V M S D C T Y H S L M O R M K J R E
K Q R I U B H A E T A S F M M D R Q J L
R E S N R E E T N R H R L B I A H A Q L
U L E L F E P G Y O M N L A C T V W H I
T S K R L N T P I F E E L E K C L E E A
Z H A S C A M I C P I R M I S E D A H S
F A L L S O F T H E O H I O C T P R K R
Y K O U N L T Y R W Z N G V R D O Z V E
X A N K U J T A T T Y L Q S E I K W S V
Z M I G V I F U T F F I D D E R A U N J
I A A Y Z K Q A T O I W O T K B G L Z N
I K H A T U E K F X P L W Q L H O X N L
A D C V Y P A L R F P X C E T A N S A G
```

Bass Lake	Lincoln	Summit Lake
Brown County	McCormick's Creek	Tippecanoe River
Chain 'O Lakes	Mounds	Turkey Run
Charlestown	Ouabache	Versailles
Clifty Falls	Pokagon	White River
Falls of the Ohio	Potato Creek	Whitewater Memorial
Fort Harrison	Shades	
Harmonie	Shakamak	
Indiana Dunes	Spring Mill	

Answer is on page 97

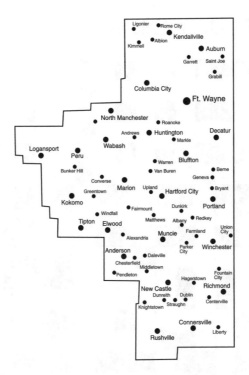

The Not-So-Far East

In the eastern part of Indiana, you'll find the hometown of one of the greatest Hollywood legends, the National Model Aviation Museum, an opalescent glass factory and "The Circus Capital of the World."

Just how did Peru, Indiana, become Circus City? Well, in 1884, the "Wallace and Company's Great World Menagerie, Grand International Mardi Gras, Highway Holiday Hidalgo and Alliance of Novelties" began spending their winter offseasons on the east bank of the Mississinewa River only two-and-a-half miles outside of town. The circus merged with other circuses and in time became the Hagenbeck-Wallace Circus, who boasted such circus stars as Emmett Kelly, Tom Mix, lion tamer Clyde Beatty and The Human Cannonball (the Great Willi Wilno).

The city still hosts a Circus City Festival each July, in which all the performers are residents of Miami County. For more information, visit their website at *www.perucircus.com.*

To-Do in Eastern Indiana

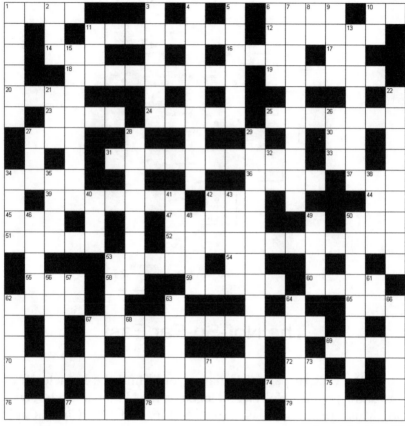

Answer is on page 97

ACROSS

1. Mistake
6. A place you can "take it on"
10. Two, to a Roman
11. James Dean's hometown ✸
12. The American Heritage Village, the Auburn Cord Duesenberg museum and the National Automative and Truck Museum of the United States ✸
14. Sally Field role: *Norma* ___

16. To be put on one's guard
17. The order these vowels go in after "c"
18. The Indiana Basketball Hall of Fame and the Wilbur Wright Birthplace & Interpretive Center ✸
19. Potatoes or rice
20. Do you ___ it? Or do you just want it?
23. The Circus Hall of Fame Museum and Professional Big Top Circus

and the Grissom Air Museum State historic Site ✷

24. "Last __ to Clarksville"
25. Not normal
27. Means of death for many an unassuming dinosaurs
30. Prefix meaning "oldest or earliest"
31. Cass County Carousel ✷
33. Symbol for indium
34. Norway's capital
36. Oops
37. Genetic blueprint
39. Salamonic Lake and Salamonic State Forest ✷
42. 1000 kilograms
44. Modifier used before a vowel
45. Someone who needs support (abbrev)
47. To ward off
50. Offer
51. Personal strength
52. Mid-America Windmill Museum ✷
53. Bovine
54. Old MacDonald's chorus vowels
55. Picabo Street's sport
58. Stereotypical exclamation
59. Amishville, USA ✷
60. Crazy
62. Book: *Goodnight* __
65. Not thin
67. Whitewater Valley Railroad ✷
69. __ Raton
70. The Indiana National Road and the Huddleston Farmhouse Inn Museum ✷
72. Short Stephen King title
74. Golf warning

76. Can be found before "Greco" and "Niño"
77. Not young
78. Wilson Vaughn Historic hostess House
79. Lewis make-believe land

DOWN

1. Zodiac twins
2. Tom Cruise flick: __ *and Away*
3. Bearcreek Farms Country Resort ✷
4. The Foellinger-Freimann Botanical Conservatory, the Lincoln Museum and the Old City Hall HIstorical Museum ✷
5. Middle english "between"
6. Gary Neuman song from the early 1980s
7. The Dan Quayle Center & Museum, and the Forks of the Wabash Historic Park✷
8. In the same place, latin
9. Nilotic people in the Sudan
10. Function word used to indicate activity
11. The cost associated with an event
13. The Hayes Regional Arboretum and the Indiana Football Hall of Fame ✷
15. The Military Armor Museum and Hoosier Park Race Track ✷
21. Guardians of the environment
22. Gaither Family Resources & Studios ✷
26. Multiple defendants, Latin
27. It is, abbreviation
28. Gene Stratton-Porter State historic Site ✷

29. Levi Coffin House State Historic Site (Indiana Underground Railroad) ★
32. Royalty (abbrev.)
34. Great Norwegian leader
35. Oz's lion (actor)
38. Something you hit on the head
40. Rap doctor
41. For heaven's _____
42. The number of Agatha Christie's Indians
43. Something desired in a court
46. Upper body
48. It's what's happening
49. Roman poet
50. Ouabache State Park ★
53. *Star Wars'* hottie
56. Opalescent Glass Factory ★

57. Not out
61. Thanks, to a Brit
62. The National Model Aviation Museum, Ball State University, and the Minnestrista Cultural Center & Oakhurst Gardens ★
63. Limberlost State Historic Site ★
64. Black Pine Animal Park
66. One of the nine muses
67. A nice shade of lipstick
68. Duchamp's famous subject on a staircase
71. French "here"
73. __-la-la
75. Guessing syllable

Fix-Up the Mixed Up

Unscramble the letters below to find the names of some of some of Indiana's more interestingly-named towns.

Animal Part Names

YEESRIDB   NKISCKBU

International Indiana

EEEBTHLHM	SORELNA	LLAVERSIES
VAYVE	ZBRALI	PHLEDI
FRDOXO	LDNAPO	AAAIELXNDR
VAEENG	UPRE	GOLAAN

Answer is on page 98

Northern Indiana

Notre Dame, the Indiana Dunes, the College Football Hall of Fame, Lake Michigan, outlet mall shopping, great golf and the Recreational Vehicle/Manufactured Housing Hall of Fame are just a few of the attractions you can take in at the northernmost part of the state.

Indiana's most famous ghost story is set at the Indiana Dunes — "Diana of the Dunes," whose real name was Alice Mabel Gray. Gray was from a wealthy Chicago family, and after attending the University of Chicago, where she was a Phi Beta Kappa, she was inspired to live a life of solitude and took herself to a shack on the shore of Lake Michigan to live a simple life... and, according to a variety of sources, skinny dip in the lake.

Gray later married a man named Paul Wilson, and they seemed to live together happily by the lake for a few years ... until a dead and charred body turned up on the beach. Wilson was questioned and released, but public opinion was against the beach dwellers. They moved to nearby Michigan City, where she died after giving birth to her second daughter. But popular legend says her spirit returned to the beach, where she had been happy for so many years. Many claim to have seen her nude ghost frolicking among the waves.

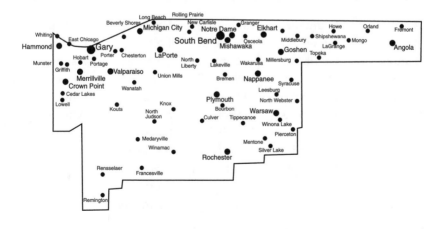

Northern Indiana Counties

```
B R Y V M O S M A D A N G V X T V T R Y
E L E P B L A K E D J O O C K J O D B X
L Q A P F R I G R A N T H W M E D U R L
E T Z C S L N R A N M P H N L U Z M H M
W S W H K A T Y W E H I E O N U V D I T
K L A P C F J P A L T T N Y Z O S R M C
J L B H I N O I L L I M R E V T T A M J
L E A F R H S R E A Y E Y A J A D W C M
X W S Y D A E Y D P M D Z T H I F O E A
L G H M N M P X K O S C I U S K O H N N
H M F O E I H H G R J P F O Q C L F Y T
C I U K H L U T N T P M N B O O N E A U
W M R J R T N O N E B U E T S C O X W P
A A H C C O T C C G F U L T O N O G Q W
P I R D M N I A T N U O F A I A F G M X
U M A R I O N S T A R K E X S H L O H N
N O B L E O G S Y R E T R O P K W M W V
I U C B E N T O N G O C I D S E I R U Y
B H Y X L L O R R A C H C O V P V S C W
J W O X R A N D O L P H S A S D U H B Y
```

Adams	Fountain	Kosciusko	Parke	Wabash
Allen	Fulton	LaGrange	Porter	Warren
Benton	Grant	LaPorte	Pulaski	Wayne
Blackford	Hamilton	Lake	Putnam	Wells
Boone	Hancock	Madison	Randolph	White
Carroll	Hendricks	Marion	Saint Joseph	Whitley
Cass	Henry	Marshall	Starke	
Clinton	Howard	Miami	Steuben	
De Kalb	Huntington	Montgomery	Tippecanoe	
Delaware	Jasper	Newton	Tipton	
Elkhart	Jay	Noble	Vermillion	

Answer is on page 98

Wander Nothern Indiana

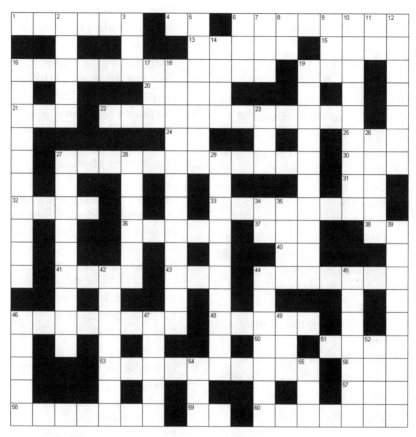

Answer is on page 100

ACROSS

1. Pokagon State Park ✷
4. Morning (abbrev)
6. Maple Wood Nature Center ✷
13. Sporting event place
15. Hip
16. The Barker Mansion and the Great Lakes Museum of Military History ✷
19. Animal doctor
20. Egyptian eyeliner
21. Scooby's family name
22. Annual Indiana Arts Expo ✷
24. The Volunteer State (abbrev)
25. Women's organization that celebrates the U.S.'s separation from British rule (abbrev.)
27. Meeno-Hof, Lambright Woodworking and Riegsecker Carriage✷
30. Is it science or is it ___?
31. Do, re, ___
32. Feeling gloomy

55

33. Amish Acres ✶
36. Banned
37. Latin for God
38. California movie star city (abbrev.)
40. Clueless exclamation: ___ if!
41. Teddy's animal-type
43. Name sponsor of the Indianapolis football stadium ✶
44. Today, I bring; yesterday, I ___
46. Beautiful sea creature also called a Devil Ray
48. Girl who adventured in wonderland
50. Also or too can be synonyms for this word
51. Insect attracted to candlelight and old sweaters
53. Indiana Dunes State Park ✶
56. O Solo ___
57. Majestic mammal with giant horns
58. John Dillinger Museum ✶
59. Titanium, on the periodic table
60. Door Prairie Auto Museum ✶

DOWN

2. Lizard seen in insurance commercials
3. Director of *Crouching Tiger, Hidden Dragon*, ___ Lee
5. Gadget
6. "___ it Be"
7. Not a specific one
8. Former prison colony (abbrev.)
9. Snoopy's alter-ego: World War I Flying ___
10. World-renowned university found in South Bend ✶
11. Don't stop!

12. The Midwest Museum of American Art and Ruthmere ✶
14. Another name for a stream
16. Deutsch Kase Haus and the Sunshine Farm ✶
17. Prefix that means "topmost" or "extreme" (from the Greek)
18. Potato Creek State Park ✶
19. The Brauer Museum of Art, the Memorial Opera House, and the Old Jail Museum ✶
23. The Mystery Machine
26. Disney's mermaid
27. College Football Hall of Fame, the Northern Indiana Center for History and the Studebaker National Museum ✶
28. Indiana Dunes National Lakeshore Visitor Center and the Dune Ridge Winery ✶
29. Billy Sunday House ✶
34. Cross off the "owed" list (abbrev.)
35. Home for partridges at Christmas time: ___ tree.
39. Unusual vegetable, often used in dips with spinach
42. Prefix meaning without government (from the Greek)
44. Then Bonneyville Mill and the Elkhart County Historical Museum ✶
45. Pet bather
46. Last name of the family in *Little Women*
47. Not behind but up ___
49. Baby noise
52. Pinball machine comment
54. Egyptian king (nickname)
55. A small bite or attempt to bite

Small Town

Puzzle by Lisa Paczkowski

So, what have you learned? Can you match the Indiana town name with the clue that describes it?

1.	Governor Otis Bowen Residence	a.	New Castle
2.	Edgar Allan ___	b.	Cicero
3.	Ski Resort: _____ Peaks	c.	Sedan
4.	James Dean's resting place	d.	Bremen
5.	Blueberry Festival site	e.	Pimento
6.	Movie treat	f.	Poe
7.	Director of *Rear Window*	g.	Swan
8.	Bart or Lisa	h.	Fairmount
9.	Indianapolis Motor _____	i.	Mitchell
10.	Amish flea market haven	j.	Paoli
11.	Former state capitol	k.	Popcorn
12.	Maxincuckee Military Academy	l.	Derby
13.	Be my _____	m.	Tyner
14.	Homeplace of Ryan White	n.	Hitchcock
15.	Indiana Basketball Hall of Fame	o.	Tyner
16.	Odd Fellows Home	p.	Simpson
17.	Remember the ____	q.	Hope
18.	Spring bulb	r.	Speedway
19.	Football-like sport	s.	Rugby
20.	To wish or want	t.	Shipshewana
21.	Small northern town established in 1855	u.	Tulip
22.	Kentucky ____	v.	Corydon
23.	Automobile	w.	Alamo
24.	Olive Stuffing	x.	Culver
25.	Long-necked bird	y.	Greensburg
26.	Hometown of astronaut Gus Grissom	z.	Valentine

Answer is on page 99

"Knee-High by the Fourth of July"

Everywhere you go in Indiana, you will see cornstalks reaching for the sky. But not all of that corn is for corn on the cob! As a matter of fact, Indiana is the number one producer of popcorn in the world!

So, the next time you go to a movie or pop up some microwave popcorn to eat on your couch, keep in mind that you are probably eating some of that Indiana corn!

One of Indiana's most famous former residents is none other than Orville Redenbacher. Orville grew up in rural Indiana and then went to the School of Agriculture at Purdue University. He worked for many years cross-breeding 30,000 varieties of popcorn before he developed his famous "gourmet" blend, which he successfully marketed and sold at the national level. His hometown of Valparaiso, IN, hosts the Popcorn Festival each year, and he was the grand marshall of the popcorn parade until his death in 1995.

Turkey Run State Park
by Sally Morge Hassler

A piece of paradise
On a hot summer day
Is the peace and tranquility
In the cool canyon way.
As the stream babbles through
Sandstone gorges formed of old
Folks now enjoy the ageless beauty
While tales of the past are told
Of wild turkeys inhabiting
The shaded canyon runs
And Pioneers and Indians
Hunting turkeys with their sons

INDIANA THINGS

Things to Do
Things to See
Things to Know

"Things"

I realize it's not the most descriptive title, but it works! Here's where you'll find puzzles about Indiana trees, birds, festivals and other "things" that are of interest about and around the Hoosier state.

A Little Indiana in the Big Apple

Dave Letterman isn't the only Hoosier import to New York. Bedford limestone was used to make one of the most famous NY landmarks. Can you figure out which one?

$\overline{}\;\overline{}\;\overline{}$ 36 3 20   6 5 14 16 35 32

26 43 23 63 37   51 77 84 21 93 89 28 66

Fill in the name of the Indiana singer/songwriter associated with each of the following songs and then use those letters to fill in the above blanks.

1. "Paper in Fire"

1 2 3 4   5 6 7 8 9 10 11 12 13 14

2. "Man in the Mirror"

15 16 17 18 19 20 21   22 23 24 25 26 27 28

3. "I Get a Kick Out of You"

29 30 31 32   33 34 35 36 37 38

4. "Control"

39 40 41 42 43   44 45 46 47 48 49 50

5. "When Can I See You"

51 52 53 54 55 56 57 58

6. "Don't it Make My Brown Eyes Blue"

— — — — — — —   — — — — —
59 60 61 62 63 64 65   66 67 68 69 70

6. "Hurt So Good" (Hint: name change)

— — — —   — — — — — —
71 72 73 74   75 76 77 78 79 80

6. "It Ain't Easy Bein' Easy"

— — — — —   — — — — — —
81 82 83 84 85   87 88 89 90 91 92

6. "Hot For Teacher"

— — — — —   — — —   — — — —
93 94 95 96 97   98 99 100   101 102 103 104

Answer is on page 100

CARDINAL REASSURANCE
by Sally Morge Hassler

Early dawn, I gaze out on a Cardinal about
To partake of a seed from a wind-tossed weed.
His beauty abounds with contrast to grounds,
Bright as a radiant sunset and yet
Timid and shy, ever ready to fly
Over yon meadow, out of reach from below.
See him soar and glide, not attempting to hide
His full coat of red, now not causing him dread.
He ascends in the air, where angels there share
A hushed cardinal word with our grand Cardinal bird.
And thus reassured, this grand Cardinal bird
Returns with a song to sing loud and long.

Indiana Birds

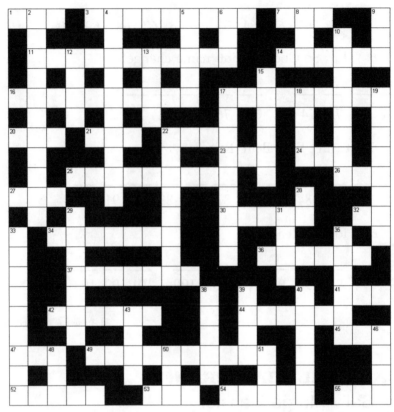

Answer is on page 101

ACROSS

1. An exclamation of discovery
3. A "safe haven" for birds
7. That's our __ in the hole.
11. "Hush, little baby, Papa's gonna buy you a _____."
14. The study of eggs
16. These viewing devices are a birdwatcher's best friend.
17. Cheery little birds, it is no wonder that they became a symbol of happiness. ★
20. Blink 182: "What's My _____ Again?"
21. Where pigs live
22. Not warm
23. Tweedle ___ and Tweedle Dum
24. Lives in a convent
25. A type of falcon that can be seen in the Hoosier state. ★
26. Break
27. "We __ the World"
30. The Canada _____ passes through Indiana twice yearly on its migratory journey. ★

32. Spanish for yes
34. The _____ Society is an excellent resource for bird-watching information.
36. A bird's toe
37. To attract goldfinches, _____ seeds are the most effective bird feed. ★
41. Every lock has a ____.
42. Although best known for their association with Baltimore, there are several varieties of this bird in Indiana. ★
44. Named for their electric blue shade, the ____ Bunting can be found in Indiana during the warm summer months. ★
45. The varities of this "wise" bird that are found in Indiana include the Great Horned and the Eastern Screech. ★
47. Opposite of Old
49. The Redneaded variety of this bird — made famous by Woody — can be found in Central Indiana. ★
52. To dive in a birdlike fashion
53. Beverage for a banquet hall
54. A four to one mixture of water and _____ is used in most hummingbird feeders.
55. "Oh, say, can you ____..."

DOWN

2. This smallest species of bird can be found in an Indiana garden.★
4. The care of birds
5. Digits
6. __, white and blue
8. A noise doves make
9. Naked as a ____ bird
10. Named for it's plaintive cry, the _____ dove can be found throughout the state. ★
12. Known for its straight flight, this big, black bird is common in Indiana. ★
13. Lady Jane ____
15. The Wild _____ was Ben Franklin's preference for the symbolic bird of the United States and is native to Indiana.★
17. Once in danger of extinction, this proud symbol of America now has several nesting areas throughout the state. ★
18. As their name suggests, these swallows are commonly found near farms: _____ Swallows. ★
19. This is often described as a "bird's-eye view" of a story.
22. Indiana's state bird ★
28. Sanitary engineering (abbrev.)
29. Known as a buzzard, the Turkey _____ can often be seen soaring over Interstate, 70 looking for carrion.★
31. No ugly duckling, the Tundra _____ is seen throughout central Indiana. ★
33. Babes in a nest
35. Although it has the same name, the Yellow-Billed ____ sounds nothing like this type of clock.★
38. Ruin
39. Down the ___
40. The best season to take up birdwatching.★
43. This web-footed bird is the largest diving bird seen in and

around Indianapolis: the Common ____.✶

46. ____ Erie in Northern Indiana is a great place to do some birdwatching.✶

48. There are many mating rituals performed by male birds to ____ the females

50. A true ____ will wait with you in the bushes for the tufted titmouse to appear.

51. Sweep it under the ____.

Let's Celebrate!

Hoosiers celebrate everything with a festival: food, birth, seasons, ethnic heritage, trees ... you name it. And if you've never been to a small-town festival, you are missing out on one of the best parts of Indiana.

There are opportunities to have your photo taken with lion cubs, performances from local dance schools, dart games and games where you throw ping-pong balls in fish bowls, carnival rides, barbershop quartets and high school bands, parades, clothing for your cement porch goose, flea markets, homemade candles, candy and coat stands and the food — oh, the food!

At the Harvest Homecoming Festival in New Albany, you can crunch tasty carmel apples with the carmel still warm. At the Little Italy Festival in Clinton, there is all-you-can-eat spaghetti. A variety of towns support an Octoberfest, with live polka music playing while you enjoy your sauerkraut and bratwurst. Not to mention the never-ending variety of street vendors that sell such delicious treats as nachos, giant pretzels, cotton candy and hand-cut french fries— all of which are guarenteed to raise your cholesterol but might just be worth it.

I had so much fun reading about the Indiana festivals that I felt two puzzles were in order: One to give you an idea of just the diversity of subjects Hoosiers celebrate with a festival; the other to see if you can put the location of the festival together with what is celebrated there. Have fun!

Celebrated In Indiana

```
                              L G K Y
                              H A D M
                              J R F S
                              G R
                              A X
                    W T M U I T Q T
                G H K N N S E S U C R I C Y T
    E W A I P R E M M U S M O O R H S U M F I R
    Q S Y C K U F S E E R T D O O W G O D L B R
    J J E F I Y V L Z A Z R L G K L Z E G O A N
    Z O N T Z O F O D R A Z I W E H T D U W S H
    S S I X K S E G D I R B D E R E V O C E T K
    A C W F L E A M A R K E T S V L D R U R L U
    M A S M O K H P U R Y S E L P A M Q Y S I D
    T R S N A E B Y V A N J C B S N I K P M U P
    S E I R R E B P S A R X R A M T S F E Q Q F
    I C W Y R O T S I H L L I M N O T T O C L R
    R R S O D S E I R R E B W A R T S N H M D U
    H O S I L J A Z Z I I A I A K M V K U G E S
    C W A R S W I N G I N G B R I D G E S R I E
    J S L L A F N O T H R E V J            U L
    G P G H T C X                          Y P
                                           N P
                                           G A
                                           P T
```

Antiques	Bridges	Maple Syrup	Swinging Bridges
Apples	Dogwood Trees	Mushrooms	Swiss Wine
Arts	Fall	Navy Beans	The Wizard of Oz
Beer	Flea Markets	Pumpkins	
Cars	Flowers	Quilts	
Christmas	Glass	Raspberries	
Circuses	Hawaiian Steel Guitars	Rodeo	
Cotton Mill	Jazz	Scarecrows	
History	Lights	Strawberries	
Covered		Summer	

Answer is on page 101

Indiana Festivals

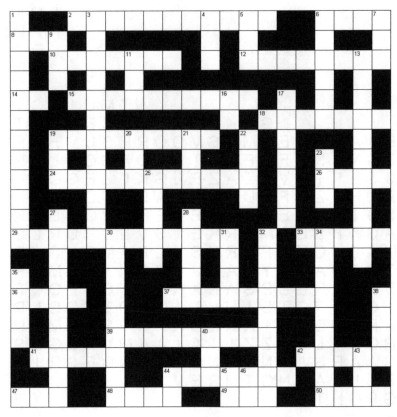

Answer is on page 102

ACROSS

2. The largest Civil War reenactment in Indiana takes place at this village every June. ✶

6. The Wabash _____ starts in Lafayette and ends in Terre Haute; participants learn about the nature and history of the river. ✶

8. ___ and sympathy

10. This southern Indiana city is host to the "Indiana Hot Luck and Fiery Foods Exhibition."✶

12. This edible fungus is found in a variety of Indiana towns and is celebrated at several local festivals. ✶

14. __ the People

15. Grown in abundance in Southwestern Indiana, Vincennes hosts a festival celebrating this summer-time treat. ✶

18. Orange County, Indiana, is famous for its spring festival that is named for this flowering tree.✶

19. This western town's hot dog festival each summer features all "dog"-related events. ✷
24. This artsy district in Indianapolis is host to an Art Fair each spring. ✷
26. This town of his birth celebrates Cole Porter each summer with a festival. ✷
29. This German spring festival takes place each April in Terre Haute. ✷
33. These cart-driving farmers are a familiar sight in our state and celebrated in the Gasthof Spring Festival in Montgomery each May. ✷
36. Middlebury's fragrant Festival of the Wild _____ Moon takes place each June. ✷
37. This film festival takes place in Indianapolis each October and recognizes films that express hope and respect for human life. ✷
39. This variety of country music is celebrated each March in Columbus. ✷
41. The whole process of making this syrup is celebrated in a variety of winter festivals throughout northern Indiana.✷
42. This drab color is a strange choice of names for the county tucked in the hills outside of Bloomington that is host to many craft and art shows. ✷
44. A professional ice-carving compeition is part of the Winter Magic Festival in this northern Indiana town. ✷

47. It's a ___ world.
48. Truth or ____
49. Opposite of happy
50. Hum

DOWN

1. These sweet fruits are celebrated at a variety of Indiana festivals, including in Rosedale and Lafayette. ✷
3. Always a big event, the State Fair happens every August in this capital city. ✷
4. Beam
5. Wahoo
6. Fiesta Cinco de Mayo is a Mexican festival, but the Indiana city hosting the biggest celebration of the day shares a name with a city in Poland. ✷
7. Kipling's novel
9. American Medical Association
11. "Oh, say, can you _____..."
13. Several cities in Indiana have their own version of this September German festival. ✷
16. Chesterton celebrates the Wizard of this make-believe land each fall. ✷
17. Van Buren, Indiana, celebrates this favorite movie food each August with a three-day event.✷
19. Short for "fabulous"
20. Baby goat
21. Popular urban music trend
22. Although they don't seem to have much to do with scratching dogs, these markets can be found almost every summer weekend in the Hoosier state.✷

23. Primate
25. Celebrated in Rochester each June, these barns have an unusual shape. ✱
27. The former home of William Henry Harrison, this Vincennes house can be toured by candlelight one night each May. ✱
28. With this small city's name, it's not hard to understand why their biggest festival is Swiss Days. ✱
30. Home to Notre Dame, this city hosts the annual College Football Hall of Fame Enshrinement Festival. ✱
31. Rip
32. This seed-spreading do-gooder has an event in Fort Wayne each fall. ✱

34. Winchester, Indiana's celebration of "Fat Tuesday" takes place in October rather than in the spring. ✱
35. People gather in the circle in downtown Indianapolis each year for the lighting of the _____, a transformed Sailors and Soldiers Monument. ✱
38. This Indiana crop is roasted and served as an all-you-can eat dish at a festival in Schererville each July. ✱
40. As part of the Indianapolis 500 festivities, there is a Rookie ____ for kids two to 13 at Monument Circle. ✱
43. To not lose
44. What about ___?
45. Secret Service
46. Short for "thanks"

Shady Fun

All of the following kinds of trees can be found in the state of Indiana, but can you find all of them in the following puzzle?

Ash	Cottonwood	Magnolia	Sourwood
Aspen	Cypress	Maple	Sweetgum
Basswood	Elm	Mulberry	Sycamore
Beech	Hackberry	Oak	Tulip
Birch	Hawthorne	Pawpaw	Walnut
Box Elder	Hemlock	Persimmon	Yellowwood
Butternut	Honeylocust	Pine	
Catalpa	Hop Hornbeam	Redbud	
Cedar	Kentucky Coffee	Sassafras	
Chestnut	Locust	Serviceberry	

Indiana Trees

```
      H T H
     B S U O W A R
    E Y N S M P D W A
    E W T R L I C H E T D
   C R S S E R P Y C O Z H E
  H S E R V I C E B E R R Y O C
  D H D W Y R R E B L U M N G R
 K C O L M E H H D G K L G F B N N
E E R T E E F F O C Y K C U T N E K E
E N I P X F B O N O A P L A T A C A S
S E E D O S W E E T G U M U H F U O M
B Y R P B S I A Y T U N R E T T U B E
 I C T S Y E L L O W W O O D R N L
 R A P A I L O N G A M T W O P
 B C M I W A C W U E Y O M A V
  B H O L C U O H T O M M U
      R U S O S D I
       E T D A S
       N W R R E
        A E F
        P D A
        W B S
        A U S
        P D A
        D Q S
```

Answer is on page 102

A Popular Tulip Poplar
by Sally Morge Hassler

Oh, the Tulip Poplar near Wabash Road
Has always been popular, or so I am told.
It was just a sapling when Indiana
became a state,
But it stands mighty tall at the present
date.
Many a man has sat in its shade,
And many a child has sat there and
played.
Many a lover has carved on dear names,
And many a mother has shared picnics and games.
Its silence has given answers to souls needing words,
And its branches have given safety to squirrels and birds.
The tree has given shelter through many a rain,
And it has given comfort to sad folks in pain.
Yes, the Tulip Poplar near Wabash Road
Has always been popular, or so I am told.
If that tree could talk, what would it say
Of life from the past and of life today?

Do You Know ...

1.) What is the Indiana state song?

2.) What is the Indiana state tree?

3.) What is the Indiana state flower?

4.) What is the Indiana state bird?

5.) What is on the Indiana state flag?

Answers on page 103

Indiana Wildlife

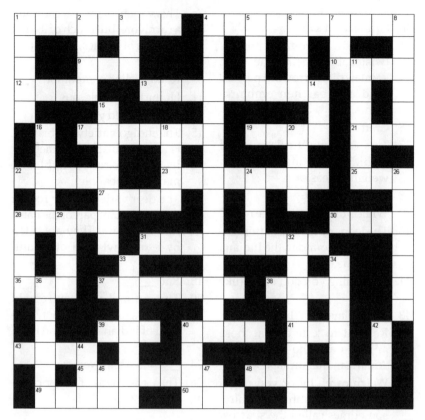

Answer is on page 103

ACROSS

1. Marshes
4. Once eliminated from Indiana, these birds were reintroduced with success to our state. ✶
9. Decay
10. Percussion section necessity
12. Mope
13. Found in the Indiana grasslands is the black swallowtail variety of this beautiful insect. ✶

17. This water animal is very common in wetland habitats throughout Indiana. ✶
19. Hobble
21. Beaver's home
22. "____ for the Holy Grail"
23. These little creatures are found in open woodlands, forest edges and bushy areas throughout Indiana. ✶
25. Aspen necessity
27. An Antigone playwright

28. The green variety of this bird lives in most of Indiana's wetland areas. ✶
30. Opposite of sad
31. Well-known from the tongue twister about their name, these animals dig burrows in pasture land and earthen embankments. ✶
35. Craft
37. This variety of turtle is found in Indiana ponds, lakes and wetland areas. ✶
38. Yellow Teletubby
39. What is meant by "on the rocks"
40. The leopard variety of this amphibian is found in the Indiana wetlands. ✶
41. Something you don't give (like a hoot).
43. Sport played on the moon
45. Related to kangaroos, these animals are the only North American marsupials. ✶
48. Watch carefully or you might miss this beautiful little bird, sometimes called the sparrow hawk. ✶
49. Poison
50. Annoy (slang)

DOWN

1. Card game
2. Frolic
3. Ready or ___, here I come!
4. These regal creatures were once eliminated from Indiana but were reintroduced in the 1940s. They are now found in most of the state. ✶
5. Shakespeare's sadly mistreated father figure
6. Duck
7. This variety of fox is technically a carnivore, but much of its diet consists of berries, grasses and nuts. ✶
8. Koko's feline companion
11. Home to the Colossus
14. A countrified yes
15. The indigo variety of this bird is actually black; it is the way its feathers reflect light that make it appear blue. ✶
16. The deer variety of this rodent is an important part of the natural food chain. They are eaten by foxes, owls and other animals. ✶
18. Rat ___
20. This animal with extremely valuable fur is a common resident of Indiana's wetland habitats. ✶
24. ___ Ado About Nothing
26. The Crossroads of America ✶
28. Wife of Zeus
29. Core
32. Bluespring Caverns and Spring Mill State Park are both home to these pigmentless crustaceans. ✶
33. Everywhere in Indiana, it seems you can find these masked bandits of the animal kingdom. ✶
34. Once found only on Indiana's northwest prairies, these nocturnal animals can now be found in central and southern Indiana as well. ✶
36. Quip
40. Mistake

42. Although they might seem bigger, the screech variety of this bird is normally less than 10 inches in height. ✶

44. The gray variety of the dog-like animal is the only such in North America that can climb trees. ✶

46. R Square

47. 12th letter of the Greek alphabet

Indiana Reservoirs

```
          X I       C R
          T Z       F M
          Z X       W M
     L    N A       G Y         G
 M I S S I S S I N E W A L A K E K U
 E B R O O K V I L L E L A K E O L E
   B S E K A L N O T G N I T N U H
   E K A L L L I M S E L G A C K A
     K S A L A M O N I E L A K E
     M U C H A R D E N L A K E W
       E K A L A K O T O P Z Y
       H A R D Y L A K E X P I
             N V C N G P
```

Brookville Lake
Cagles Mill Lake
Harden Lake
Hardy Lake

Huntington Lake
Mississinewa Lake
Potoka Lake
Salamonie Lake

Answer is on page 104

Pieces of Hoosier History

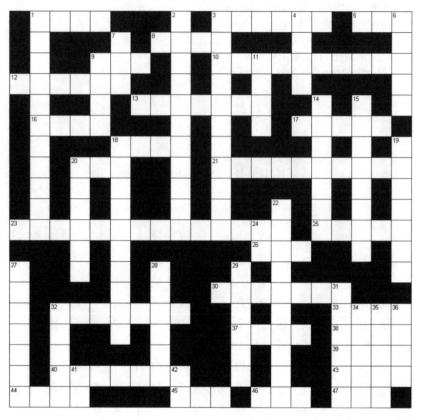

Answer is on page 104

ACROSS

1. Indiana's largest cash crop ★
3. Indiana astronaut Gus Grissom is a graduate of this institution of higher learning. ★
5. Bird
8. This river forms the southern border of Indiana. ★
9. American pub
10. Birthplace of labor leader and socialist Eugene V. Debs. ★
12. Hometown of Jimmy Hoffa, who might or might not be buried under Giants' Stadium. ★
13. This Indiana author was the governor of the New Mexico territory from 1878 to 1881: Lew _____. ★
16. Anna _____: the Indiana native and John Dillinger's betrayer, "The Lady in Red" ★
17. Number of interstate highways in Indiana. ★

18. Honeymakers
20. Central Intelligence Agency (abbrev.)
21. William Henry Harrison's campaign slogan: "_____ and Tyler Too." *
23. Indiana city that is home to the world's second-largest clock. *
25. Spaghetti sauce maker
26. Hedwig, Harry's pet
30. "Patriot Priest of the Old Northwest": Father Pierre _____. *
32. This president lay in state at the Indianapolis state capitol building on April 30, 1865. *
33. Spoken
37. Term
38. Starling
39. Ripe
40. Indiana inventor of the rapidfire gun: something "to make war so terrible that nations would want to turn against it."*
43. Ceramic ___
44. Light
45. Evil creature from Tolkien world
46. Ta-ta
47. Keats: "___ on a Grecian Urn"

DOWN

1. The starting point for the Lewis and Clark expedition was in this Indiana town. *
2. This southern Indiana town was the site of the first governor of Indiana's inaugural ball. *
3. This Native American tribe was escorted out of Indiana to reservations in Kansas in 1838.*
4. Second-hand

6. The ___ Botanical Gardens features 13 acres of rugged glacier-made ridges with native trees and wildflowers. *
7. Friend
9. Nip
11. Spin
14. This famous Presbyterian minister held his first pastorate in Lawrenceburg from 1837 to 1839: Henry Ward ___. *
15. First governor of Indiana: Jonathon_____. *
18. In 1838, this financial disaster befell the state of Indiana. *
19. Limestone from this Indiana town was used to build the Empire State Building. *
20. Indiana abolitionist and key participant in the Indiana Underground Railroad. *
22. The Smithsonian Institute can trace its origins to this Indiana town. *
24. ___ and behold
27. Indiana was the number-one producer of this snack food in 1992
28. Who was the president of the U.S. when Indiana's Thomas Riley Marshall served two terms as vice-president? *
29. State flower of Indiana from 1931 to 1957 *
31. This canned juice was first produced in Kokomo, Indiana. *
32. Slang
34. Taut
35. Anoint
36. Dip
41. Above-named
42. Wend

Indiana Colleges and Universities

```
N C T H N J R G J O Z C T I M A R I A N C O L L E G E G S K
J Q H H A E Z B H A W A B A S H C O L L E G E J K M Q C V G
U P U R D U E U N I V E R S I T Y E G E L L O C E C A R G R
U A N A I D N I N R E H T U O S F O Y T I S R E V I N U U V
N F D Z W S U N I V E R S I T Y O F S A I N T F R A N C I S
I D D S I Y T D E L L I V S N A V E F O Y T I S R E V I N U
V A L P A R A I S O U N I V E R S I T Y T N Y P Q E M J D E
E U M G E X E A A B A L L S T A T E U N I V E R S I T Y I G
R N R M F H X N K N E G E L L O C R E T S E H C N A M Z A E
S I A S L P A A T Y K T C H A N O V E R C O L L E G E N L
I V M A H J I I B E T H E L C O L L E G E O G G B Y Z V A L
T E C I H E Z N W A N D E R S O N U N I V E R S I T Y D S O
Y R A N I M E S L A C I G O L O E H T A I D R O C N O C T C
O S Q T B T V T D I Y H X D L G O S H E N C O L L E G E A S
F I J M C N C I W U E G E L L O C T E M U L A C A F Q N T H
I T E A V Q S T B K P A A A M Y G W D A N V C W G B M S E P
N Y K R X Q E U K B Y T I S R E V I N U A N A I D N I H U E
D O G Y H Q A T R M Z M S M V V T E C K Y G R N U I F Z N S
I F I S P Z Z E G E L L O C M A H L R A E G I R L L J Z I O
A N H C E T F O E T U T I T S N I N A M L U H E S O R D V J
N O B O U A W F Z M Z C L H O L Y C R O S S C O L L E G E T
A T C L H U N T I N G T O N C O L L E G E F E Q A X Y B R N
P R O L L E G E L L O C N I L K N A R F W R D M J Z P H S I
O E G E L L O C S D O O W E H T F O Y R A M T N I A S L I A
L D J G P F K H Q A K W J U D M W Z U F N M V G P N X H T S
I A T E A X L N Y T I S R E V I N U W U A P E D Z E A Y Y Z
S M E T A Y L O R U N I V E R S I T Y D I W G S M L Z R T B
I E X Y B U T L E R U N I V E R S I T Y D E X B R V Z I Y B
B J E H X Z L O O A K L A N D C I T Y U N I V E R S I T Y W
K H Y Q P E G G N N T R I S T A T E U N I V E R S I T Y D P
```

Answer is on page 105

Anderson University
Ball State University
Bethel College
Butler University
Calumet College
Christian Theological Seminary
Concordia Theological Seminary
DePauw University
Earlham College
Franklin College
Goshen College

Grace College
Hanover College
Holy Cross College
Huntington College
Indiana Institute of Technology
Indiana State University
Indiana University
Indiana Wesleyan University
Manchester College
Marian College
Oakland City University

Purdue University
Rose Hulman Institute of Technology
Saint Joseph's College
Saint Mary-of-the-Woods Colleg
Saint Mary's College
Taylor University
TriState University

University of Evansville
University of Indianapolis
University of Notre Dame
University of Saint Francis
University of Southern Indiana
Valparaiso University
Wabash College

Famous Alumni

Match the following celebrities with their Indiana alma mater:

Dave Letterman

Kevin Kline

Larry Bird

Neil Armstrong

Hannah Storm

Dan Quayle

Indiana University

Purdue University

Ball State University

University of Notre Dame

DePauw University

Indiana State University

Answer is on page 105

77

Indiana Newspapers

We've given you the name of the paper. Can you give us the name of the town it is published in? Answer is on page 106.

ACROSS

1. *The Star Press* ★
4. *News-Examiner* ★
9. *Purdue Exponent* ★
10. ____ de Triumph
13. "There She Goes" band
14. *Banner-Graphic* ★
16. Simpson judge
17. Detour
19. _____ into a false sense of security
20. Hippie wish
23. "___ He's a Jolly Good Fellow"
24. Angelina Jolie flick: ____ *Raider*
26. Alarm company
28. *The News Dispatch* ★
29. *The News-Sun* ★
31. *Daily Citizen* ★

34. Grant monogram in *North by Northwest*
35. *Times Sentinel* ★
37. A craving
38. Monkey's cousin
40. *Herald-Argus* ★
41. *Tribune-Star* ★
42. Not any
43. Mailed
44. Not them

DOWN

2. Bird's house
3. *The Crescent Online* ★
4. *Journal Review* ★
5. Word sometimes used to mean "name at birth"
6. To consume
7. *Star/News* ★
8. The opposite of most
9. *Times-Herald* ★
11. *Chesterton Tribune* ★
12. Temporary office help
14. *Post-Tribune* ★
15. *The Post & Mail* ★
18. *Journal and Courier* ★
21. Tasty fish
22. Movie about baby boomers: *The Big* _____
25. *Today in Batesville & Oldenburg* ★
27. *Madison Courier* ★
30. *Democrat* ★
32. Back of the neck
33. Native American
35. Country with capital city of Kinshasa
36. "A serious _____ of judgment"
38. Beck: "Where it's _____. I've got two turntables and a microphone."
39. *The Peru Tribune* ★
41. Maker of Beanie Babies

Bizarre Indiana

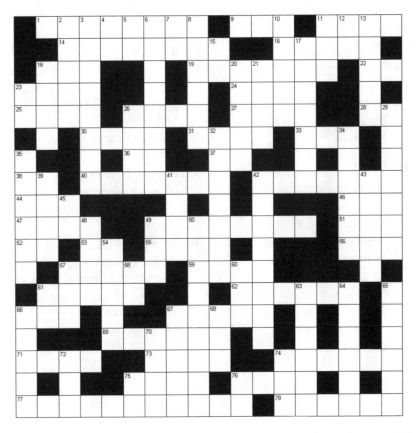

Answer is on page 106

ACROSS

1. The Indiana record for continuous playing of _____ and Dragons is 120 hours and was set by six high-school students in 1982. ✷

9. Exclamation of discovery

11. Giant automaker

14. Adjective applied to a potato

16. 1996 movie starring Geoffrey Rush as classical pianist David Helfgott.

18. Dickensian hero

19. The longest trip taken on this type of vehicle by a Hoosier is 2500 miles (from Georgia to California). ✷

22. Football point-getter (abbrev.)

23. A channel through which a substance is conveyed

24. Paddington Bear's birthplace: Darkest _____

25. One who speaks Siamese

26. Ball State University was host

to the biggest Indiana group
_____ ; 3400 persons all left the
ground together in 1980. ⋆
27. Walking heavily
28. Fine
30. Prefix meaning defective
31. Popular seasoning
33. Pigment suitable for writing
36. Thanks, to an Englishman
37. Cerium, on the periodic table
38. A name I call myself
40. Water ice, to which milk, egg
white or gelatin is added before
freezing
42. Ted Hamilton performed nine
of these strength exercises us-
ing only one finger to set the
record for most performed in
Indiana.⋆
44. Baseball poem: "Casey at the
___"
46. 22nd letter of the Greek alphabet
47. Cleopatra's means of suicide
49. The longest game of this sport
was played for 56 innings to
raise money for Lawrence
North High School in 1983. ⋆
51. A relation
52. A drop of golden sun
53. Not for viewers under the age
of 17: ___-17
55. Swiss mountain range
56. To droop
57. Canadian bump in the road
59. Abbreviation used on memos
61. The longest chain made of this
flimsy substance in Indiana
was 15 miles, 230 yards. ⋆
62. Lee Hyland of Marion County

smoked 28 of these at one time
to set Indiana's record for the
most.⋆
66. To prohibit
67. Charlie or Martin
69. Clean yet? David A. Hoffman
took the longest one of these in
Indiana: 174 hours. ⋆
71. Adjective used to describe
Cinderella's stepsisters
73. French head
74. Kentucky coffee tree
75. An entry in law staying all pro-
ceedings in an action (abbrev.)
76. Cat's approval sound
77. Hoosier David Williams was
the national champion for this
"hip" event in 1972. ⋆
78. Not present

DOWN

2. Manufacturing New York town
also a small river town in IN ⋆
3. The highest one of these in
Indiana was performed in
Evansville in 1906 at the top of
a newly errected smokestack. ⋆
4. Home of Prince Charles
(abbrev.)
5. Type of engineer (abbrev.)
6. A descriptive words that means
to tell someone something in a
solemn or obscure fashion
7. Forbidding word
8. To set the Indiana record for
most continous _____, you'd
have to beat Tim Wood's record
of 15,325, set at the Jordan
YMCA in 1973. ⋆
10. The Jetsons' dog
11. Evergreen

12. Not off
13. Return to popularity of a previous style
15. Someone to visit when you are sick (abbrev.)
17. Bill Shirk, who has been called a modern-day _____, has perfomed more than 17 "escapes" to set the Indiana record.★
18. New Zealand spice
20. The world record for picking this fruit is held by George Adrian of Waverly, Indiana. He picked 365.5 bushels in eight hours. ★
21. A modern Gael
23. To do something twice as fast (abbrev.)
26. A French jump
29. Dino DeLorean and Barbara Kane hold the Indiana record for this event: 21 days. ★
32. Jodie Foster or Julia Roberts
34. A marbles game
35. To set off, as on a long journey
39. A state of being comfortable
41. A golden-colored Madiera wine
42. 15 hours, 6 minutes is the Indiana record for hand _____ which was set in 1973. ★
43. Evil scientist's glass container
45. Bathroom essential (abbrev.)
48. An abrupt closing

49. A vampire's alter-ego
50. Lynn Helms set the Indiana record for sitting in this type of wet pasta in 1981 when she sat for 68 hours. ★
54. The longest single match of this board game in Indiana was played for 168 hours by Ilya Schwartzman and Stan Zygmunt. ★
57. This type of container was stacked 25 feet, three inches (7000 items) high in July 1976 to raise money for the Valparaiso First Church of the Nazarene. ★
58. Goes with either
60. High card
61. Ma's husband
63. To take it all in
64. 2056 pounds of soft serve ice cream and 17 gallons of syrup went into making this Indiana record-holding sweet treat. ★
65. To please
66. Magazine workplace that is the setting for "Just Shoot Me"
67. To brush off
68. Before (middle english)
70. Attar
72. Internet equivalent of "HA!"
74. Women's undergarment
75. Say it isn't ___.
76. A youth might need a chaperone to a movie with this rating (abbrev.).

Made in Indiana

```
T N E Y Z Q Q X U G J V L R Q S N X H W O U Q U H P J M C Y
A N W J J L Y S P H L C H O M E F R E E Z E R S T C O N S A
X Y I B R P F Q V I P K O A O N V L B I X K R E P C J A V M
V O M E B B H R I U N K M W G I X P O Z Z U V N A T Z H V F
L Y N J J G Q M P C T S E W L G X U G D B Y I I I G A L I J
D G A Z C T W Y S Q U I R F B N D K K B E U W G A U Y H R Z
F S L U T L S E L X P E E D B E Z P E U V N H N O W O P M I
T C E M A M H Q P A A I F L A T A R O U Y A U E U U Z S E S
P J E I M P B T Z M Z B R Z Q F G N U O P O M L S K P U I D
R U U T D R E C R E A T I O N A L V E H I C L E S F A K R W
O K R Q T O C R Z K S U D D S R B L V R X I H S Q H L Q T D
V G A I E C B A T D H P G K P C I I A Y Z O O E W J U V M S
U V J E P E M S R S T N E M U R T S N I L A C I S U M X S W
J C Y H M S A C U E Y T R S G I F D S D B P E D C H I E N J
S T D G Z S V Z C B S E A D O A N D A D G S E I K U N B P M
Z J Y J T E F C K N A I T I E R U U B G U P T M C Y U S L Y
K W K T P D N G B E I Y E M K N D T T M K I F E W L M L A T
L L E L E C T R O N I C R E S I S T O R S H H S E Z P A S I
P V A F M O F Q D N B X S D O L K Q Q M U C I R D L R C T N
K P N U E R U T I N R U F E C I F F O D O O W O S M O I I P
Z H T R T N U W E Y V K Q E D T S O C Z S T I T O N D T C G
I V M X A P L K S O I U O N B C N Y D L P A I A Y C U U P P
O K I C L R S S G N I R A E B L L A B N Y T M V B W C E R H
T T N W D O O U E P T M O V F V N G D N C O X E E O T C O V
H A T R O D W P M T I G X O D C P V J P T P N L A P S A D A
S Q M H O U S E H O L D V I D E O E Q U I P M E N T A M U U
D P H Q R C N K A X B P C X U B I K V H K K Y D O T G R C L
Z I U X S T P S H H K A J N I F Q X Q J N P G H I Z R A T J
W F F C W S P O M E O K X U C G I N U F M R L J L N H H S S
U X B X Z C Q A P X W G C J D W B J E L K K I C L O L P V V
```

Did you know that all of these items were made in Indiana?

Aircraft Engines	Household Audio	Processed Corn
Aluminum Products	Equipment	Products
Automotive Parts	Household Video	Recreational Vehicles
Ball Bearings	Equipment	Rubber Gaskets
Bus Bodies	Metal Doors	Semidiesel Engines
Diesel Engines	Musical Instruments	Soybean Oil
Electronic Resistors	Pharmaceuticals	Steel
Elevators	Plastic Products	Truck Bodies
Home Freezers	Popcorn	Wood Office Furniture
Home Refrigerators	Potato Chips	

Answer is on page 107

83

Indiana Crime and Punishment

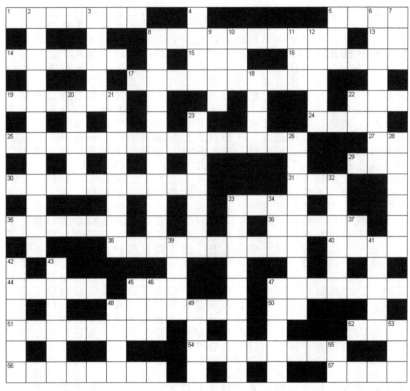

Answer is on page 107

ACROSS

1. Mt. Everest conquerer
5. Bartlett's fruit
8. Jocko Dooley was tried in 1905 for violating Indiana's no-smoking law. He had a habit of 200 cigarettes per day, but he was also nonhuman — what was he? ✯
13. Radium, on the periodic table
14. Something to live up to
15. Sara ____: famous cheesecake maker
16. Just plain mean
17. Indiana serial killer caught when the bodies of more than 11 men were discovered on his property ✯
19. This murderer's ties to Indiana include being sent to the Gibault School for Boys in Terre Haute and the Indiana School for Boys. ✯
22. It's only a number
24. Cronus' wife
25. Indiana's first electric chair was created from this other grisly

84

means of dispatching criminals. ✶

27. Yes, ___, maybe so

29. Consumed

30. Wingate, Indiana, saw the nation's first detective association that specialized in catching this 19th century criminal.✶

31. Jim Jones, famous for this "Jonestown Massacre," was born in this small Indiana burg.✶

33. Femme fatale from *The Avengers*

35. Aerial photos are used to make these accurate charts.

36. A person's circumference

38. This KKK Grand Dragon rose to power in Indiana before being convicted of second-degree murder in 1925. ✶

40. Born Romain de Tirtoff in imperial St. Petersburg, this artist had a major influence on the style and design of the 20th century.

44. Pop musician from the 1980s who sang "Caribbean Queen."

45. Casing (abbrev.)

47. This Indiana town was the site of the very first moving train robbery. ✶

48. This northern Indiana city was home to the state's most notorious murderess, Belle Gunness — killer of at least 14 men. ✶

50. Either's partner

51. Gem-cutter

52. Sadly, Indiana politics and history were largely affected by this racist organization until the

mid 1920s. ✶

54. The penalty applied to wife beaters after an 1891 act of the Indiana General Assembly. ✶

56. The type of circus animal involved in the weirdest Indiana traffic accident. ✶

57. Norse God

DOWN

2. This city was the site of the nation's first prison built for women and run by women. ✶

3. Harpy

4. Camera necessity

5. Mightier than the sword

6. Stuck-up

7. Lemonheads record: *It's a Shame About* _____

8. This southern Indiana town was the site of the very first Indiana state prison. ✶

9. Earth-inheritors

10. Dog: Shar ___

11. Greek girl's name meaning "Life"

12. Mistake

18. Han from Star Wars

20. Lover's talk

21. Direct flights

22. Latin age (abbrev.)

23. Popular Indiana fishing conquest

26. Notorious depression-era bank robber from Mooresville, Indiana. ✶

28. Body of work

32. Upper surface of a bird's body

33. This Indiana town was the site of the first execution in the na-

tion of a white man convicted of killing a Native American. ✷

34. Freud's idea of "self"

37. Your starting class in high school (abbrev.)

39. A bouncy stick

41. Winnie Ruth Judd of Indiana went on to noteriety as the "___ murderess," although she only shot the victims. Someone else chopped them up and stowed them in this. ✷

42. The strangest Indiana traffic accident was when a motorist hit an elephant who had been set free to escape a fire at the circus. Her name? ✷

43. Music term: Always

45. Automobile

46. Bill Cosby series: "I ___ "

47. Adjective used in the band's name in the movie *O Brother, Where Art Thou?*

48. Girlfriend from Dr. Zhivago

49. Floating platform

53. Barbie's trusty date

55. Green light

ANSWERS

I hope you enjoyed these puzzles and that you learned a few things as you went through the book. This is only a little bit of all the wonderful things you can learn about the great state of Indiana. Go out and learn some more!

Hoosier Greats, p. 2

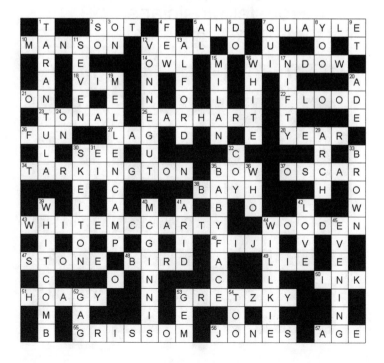

James Whitcomb Riley, p. 5

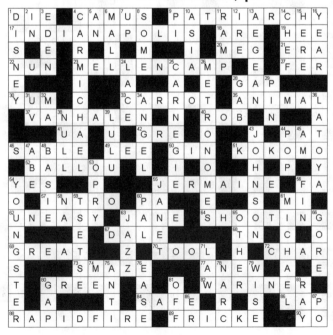

Hoosier Musicians, p. 9

Hoosiers in the Arts, p. 13

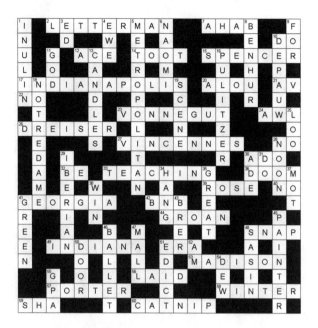

Movies Made in Indiana, p. 16

```
L E D J B X Y U P M L M B Z O E T U K Y
Y A D I L O H Y N N H O J Y S W R K E J
A P I P U T U O N E M T H G I E O T E S
W I R U E F B R I A N S S O N G H H R D
E E J S C O L V M C Q K C O Y O S E C N
H C K H H R P A Z I L Y O D O J L R S E
T E L E I C D U F J K S A S A L J Y S I
L O L D P I W X I A D L I W I J B A A R
A F D T S K X N C E A E B K I V F N R F
A E S O M E C A M E R U N N I N G W G R
G D N O R T T A S S U R U P Z A N H N U
N E M F O Y N A P M O C E H T N I I I O
I N Q A C L E E K B X R W R P A T T N F
O I Z R R L E U L J T A W R U K P E A G
G R V I P D F A Y C M I A Z G D I S M N
M G G O W B R E A K I N G A W A Y T T M
S A T A A U X L L M C M P S D K Y O S R
A N Y B T Q U F F E Q A S O M A C R E A
R E C A R G M O R F G N I L L A F Y B M
S Z N W O R I E H T F O E U G A E L A M
```

Hoosier Stars of TV and Film, p. 17

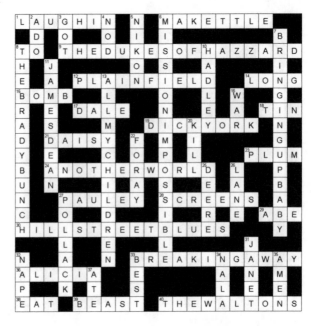

Winners of the Indianapolis 500, p. 19

The Indianapolis Speedway, p. 20

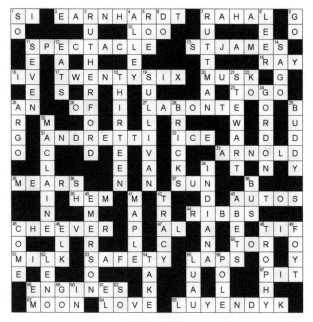

Indiana Sports Teams, p. 23

Indiana Sports, p. 24

Permanent Residents of Indiana, p. 26

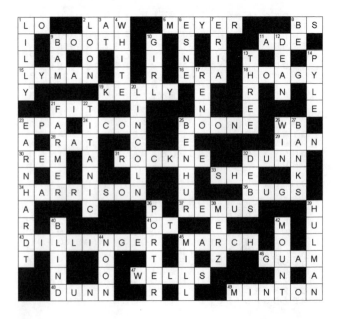

Indianapolis Attractions, p. 31

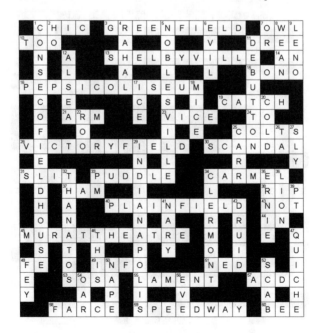

```
L I X H C I N E D O M E T H E A T E R Y O
T P N C O N S E C O F I E L D H O U S E J
M O A D I D K Z Z T I N J C G V L W X I K
H O Y A I I K Z T Q S G Z X R S X F R F F
C Z R E G A L L I V E L P P I R D A O R B
M S E R H N N A G F R E M T Q I D M U I F
L I N D I A N A W A R M E M O R I A L A A
G L I T M S R N S V V I V H Y Z K S P V K
K O W L A T B A R T S G A R D E N U S U I
Z P Y F X A Z U V R A C E W A Y P A R K M
S A E N T T T Y T X F T A L P E C Y J X X
R N L T H E C H I L D R E N S M U S E U M
Z A S Q E M M Y S T E R Y C A F E R K H I
O I A Z A U T G N Z F R W F A E I C Q H J
J D E Q T S Z S O D M Q H K V P V D J O U
T N L Y E E L L A H S E W O L C I I U O B
O I J O R U A W A G U N C E U U M T A G K
M U E S U M G R O J L E T I E S J Z O N U
E X W H I T E R I V E R G A R D E N S L L
J Q R E R A U Q S N I A T N U O F A F O Z
Z R C W G H O S I K B Q D W S A B H L B H
```

Central Indiana Wonders, p. 32

	¹C	H	I	C		³G	R	E	⁵E	N	⁶F	I	⁸E	L	D		⁷O	⁸W	⁹L
¹⁰T	O	O				A			O		V				¹¹D	R	E	E
	N		¹²A			¹³S	H	E	L	B	Y	V	I	L	L	E		¹⁴A	N
	S		L			A		L		L					¹⁵B	O	N	O
¹⁶P	E	P	S	I	C	O	L	¹⁷I	S	E	U	¹⁸M			U			
	C		E			C		S		I		¹⁹C	A	²⁰T	C	H		
	O		²¹A	²²R	M		E		²³V	I	C	E		²⁴T	O			
	F			O			I		E			²⁵C	O	²⁶L	T	²⁷S		
²⁸V	I	C	T	O	R	Y	F	²⁹I	E	L	D		³⁰S	C	A	N	D	A	L
	E			N			L			R			Y
³¹S	L	I	³²T		³³P	U	D	D	L	E		³⁴C	A	R	M	³⁵E	³⁶L
	D		³⁷H	A	M		I			L				³⁵R	I	³⁸P
	H		A			⁴⁰P	L	A	⁴¹I	N	F	I	E	L	⁴²D	⁴³N	O	T
	O		N				N		A		R		R		⁴⁴I	N
⁴⁵M	U	R	A	T	⁴⁶T	H	E	A	T	R	E		M	U	E		⁴⁷Q
	S		T		H			P		Y		O		I		U
⁴⁸F	E		O	⁴⁹I	⁵⁰N	F	O				⁵¹N	E	D	⁵²S		I
E			⁵³S	⁵⁴O	S	A		⁵⁵L	A	⁵⁶M	E	N	T		⁵⁷A	C	D	C
Y			A		P			I		V				A	H
		⁵⁸F	A	R	C	E		⁵⁹S	P	E	E	D	W	A	Y		⁶⁰B	E	E

93

Indiana High School Nicknames, p. 34

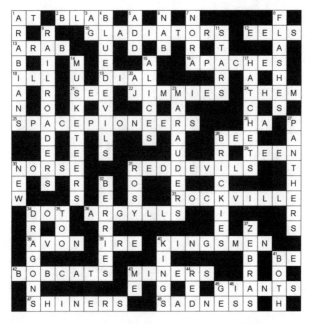

Sightseeing in Southern Indiana, p. 38

Southern Indiana Counties, p. 40

```
M A S L R F V L N E C S G N I N N E J G
M H Z F Y S L U A O J S Q W G R E E N E
D U B S S T W M V O S E D Y O L F V Q N
Z M M A K I E B I G V I R B K F P N O F
I Z Y K E K O Y L M W V R A E H E E K F
N Y O L J O W B L D N A L R E Z T I W S
A L E S K B W D U O E D S T A Z L E P S
K P N A V A Y R S D L O T H A H M C S G
K G S O Q K U N I O N E W O I H O V B P
B I A U L S H E L B Y N I L K N A R F I
H C X Q H O H W J A C K S O N N G U N K
X X B N J U D S F M E R W M D Y H T R E
H Q E P J H Y S Y T E O A E Q A A A O G
J B X Y R R E P E C N E R W A L L C W N
X B X T E M S F N W L B R N F C X E F A
J C D O S L O E O O U V I G O O W D U R
S K U B C U P R J R H T C E J M R Q W O
R G F N O S B I G S R X K N O X G D R A
J A H R T L X H R A R N O N Y S O T Z V
M U K D T L P P M H N N S X L W X M O N
```

South Central Indiana Highlights, p. 42

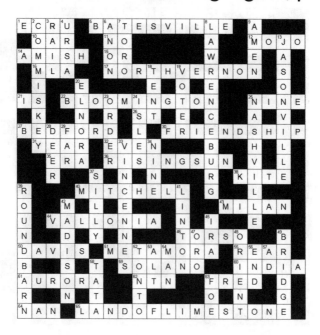

State Historic Sites, p. 44

Western Indiana Attractions, p. 46

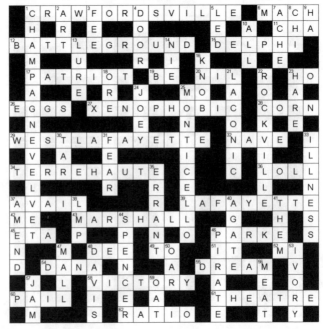

Indiana State Parks, p. 48

```
W D O W H S P R I N G M I L L Q O C I N
X H M N B Y T N U O C N W O R B Z N V I
F T I I P T O C L S D U L J V R L H X P
N F I T B D U Y J I M E W S M O C R T J
U L D P E M A E A R S H I D C J Y O N T
R S F M P W B N B R S U T N C Z H V J R
Y E A U S E A A C A M U I U O V P L M S
E E V M S D C T Y H S L M O R M K J R E
K Q R I U B H A E T A S F M M D R Q J L
R E S N R E E T N R H R L B I A H A Q L
U L E L F E P G Y O M N L A C T V W H I
T S K R L N T P I F E E L E K C L E E A
Z H A S C A M I C P I R M I S E D A H S
F A L L S O F T H E O H I O C T P R K R
Y K O U N L T Y R W Z N G V R D O Z V E
X A N K U J T A T T Y L Q S E I K W S V
Z M I G V I F U T F F I D D E R A U N J
I A A Y Z K Q A T O I W O T K B G L Z N
I K H A T U E K F X P L W Q L H O X N L
A D C V Y P A L R F P X C E T A N S A G
```

To-Do in Eastern Indiana, p. 50

Fix-Up the Mixed Up, p. 52

Animal Part Names

Birdseye   Buckskin

International Indiana

Bethlehem	Orleans	Versailles
Vevay	Brazil	Delphi
Oxford	Poland	Alexandria
Geneva	Peru	Angola

Northern Indiana Counties, p. 54

```
B R Y V M O S M A D A N G V X T V T R Y
E L E P B L A K E D J O O C K J O D B X
L Q A P F R I G R A N T H W M E D U R L
E T Z C S L N R A N M P H N L U Z M H M
W S W H K A T Y W E H I E O N U V D I T
K L A P C F J P A L T T N Y Z O S R M C
J L B H I N O I L L I M R E V T T A M J
L E A F R H S R E A Y E Y A J A D W C M
X W S Y D A E Y D P M D Z T H I F O E A
L G H M N M P X K O S C I U S K O H N N
H M F O E I H H G R J P F O Q C L F Y T
C I U K H L U T N T P M N B O O N E A U
W M R J R T N O N E B U E T S C O X W P
A A H C C O T C C G F U L T O N O G Q W
P I R D M N I A T N U O F A I A F G M X
U M A R I O N S T A R K E X S H L O H N
N O B L E O G S Y R E T R O P K W M W V
I U C B E N T O N G O C I D S E I R U Y
B H Y X L L O R R A C H C O V P V S C W
J W O X R A N D O L P H S A S D U H B Y
```

Small Town, p. 57

1. y
2. f
3. j
4. h
5. o
6. k
7. n
8. p
9. r
10. t
11. v
12. x
13. z
14. b
15. a
16. c
17. w
18. u
19. s
20. q
21. d
22. l
23. m
24. e
25. g
26. i

Wander Northern Indiana, p. 55

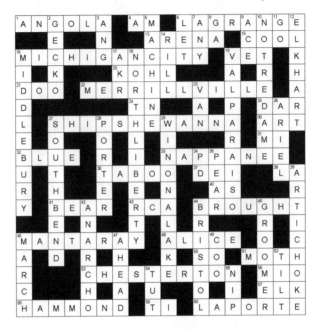

A Little Indiana in the Big Apple, p. 60

Answer: The Empire State Building

1. John Mellencamp
2. Michael Jackson
3. Cole Porter
4. Janet Jackson
5. Babyface
6. Crystal Gayle
7. John Cougar
8. Janie Fricke
9. David Lee Roth

Indiana Birds, p. 62

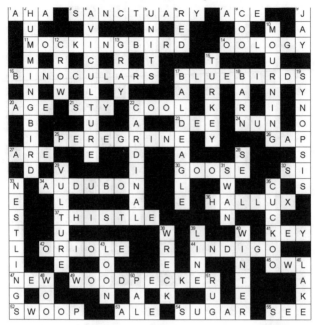

Celebrated in Indiana, p. 65

Indiana Festivals, p. 66

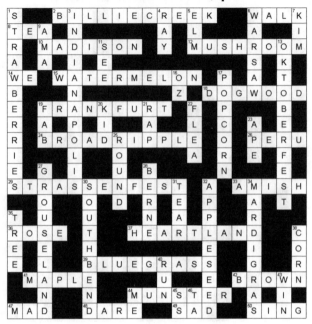

Indiana Trees, p. 69

Do You Know ..., p. 70

1. "On the Banks of the Wabash"

2. The Tulip Poplar

3. Peony

4. Cardinal

5. A Yellow Torch on a Blue Background

Indiana Wildlife, p. 71

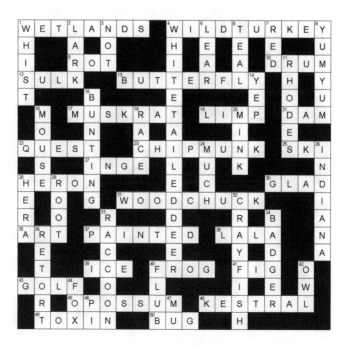

Indiana Reservoirs, p. 73

```
        X  I        C  R
        T  Z        F  M
        Z  X        W  M
     L     N  A     G  Y              G
 (M  I  S  S  I  S  S  I  N  E  W  A  L  A  K  E) K  U
 E (B  R  O  O  K  V  I  L  L  E  L  A  K  E) O  L  E
   B  S (E  K  A  L  N  O  T  G  N  I  T  N  U  H)
 (E  K  A  L  L  L  I  M  S  E  L  G  A  C) K  A
   K (S  A  L  A  M  O  N  I  E  L  A  K  E)
   M  U  C (H  A  R  D  E  N  L  A  K  E) W
     (E  K  A  L  A  K  O  T  O  P) Z  Y
     (H  A  R  D  Y  L  A  K  E) X  P  I
        N  V  C  N  G  P
```

Pieces of Hoosier History, p. 74

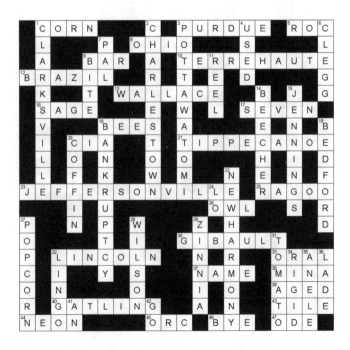

Indiana Colleges and Universities, p. 76

```
N C T H N J R G J O Z C T I M A R I A N C O L L E G E G S K
J Q H H A E Z B H A W A B A S H C O L L E G E J K M Q C V G
U P U R D U E U N I V E R S I T Y E G E L L O C E C A R G R
U A N A D N I N R E H T U O S F O Y T I S R E V I N U U V
N F D Z W S U N I V E R S I T Y O F S A I N T F R A N C I S
I D D S I Y D E L L I V S N A V E F O Y T I S R E V I N U
V A L P A R A I S O U N I V E R S I T Y T N Y P Q E M J D E
E U M G E X E A A B A L L S T A T E U N I V E R S I T Y I G
R N R M F H X N K N E G E L L O C R E T S E H C N A M Z A E
S I A S L P A A T Y T K T C H A N O V E R C O L L E G E N L
I V M A H J I I B E T H E L C O L L E G E O G G B Y Z V A L
T E C I H E Z N W A N D E R S O N U N I V E R S I T Y D S O
Y R A N I M E S L A C I G O L O E H T A I D R O C N O C T C
O S Q T B T V T D I Y H X D L G O S H E N C O L L E G E A S
F I J M C N C I W U E G E L L O C T E M U L A C A F Q N T H
I T E A V Q S T B K P A A A M Y G W D A N V C W G B M S E P
N Y K R X Q E U K B Y T I S R E V I N U A N A I D N I H U E
D O G Y H Q A T R M Z M S M V V T E C K Y G R N U I F Z N S
I F I S P Z Z E G E L L O C M A H L R A E G I R L L J Z I O
A N H C E T F O E T U T I T S N I N A M L U H E S O R D V J
N O B O U A W F Z M Z C L H O L Y C R O S S C O L L E G E T
A T C L H U N T I N G T O N C O L L E G E F E Q A X Y B R N
P R O L L E G E L L O C N I L K N A R F W R D M J Z P H S I
O E G E L L O C S D O O W E H T F O Y R A M T N A S L I A
L D J G P F K H Q A K W J U D M W Z U F N M V G P N X H T S
I A T E A X L N Y T I S R E V I N U W U A P E D Z E A Y Y Z
S M E T A Y L O R U N I V E R S I T Y D I W G S M L Z R T B
I E X Y B U T L E R U N I V E R S I T Y D E X B R V Z I Y B
B J E H X Z L O O A K L A N D C I T Y U N I V E R S I T Y W
K H Y Q P E G G N N T R I S T A T E U N I V E R S I T Y D P
```

Famous Alumni, p. 77

David Letterman, Ball State University
Kevin Kline, Indiana University
Larry Bird, Indiana State University
Neil Armstrong, Purdue University
Hannah Storm, University of Notre Dame
Dan Quayle, DePauw University

Indiana Newspapers, p. 78

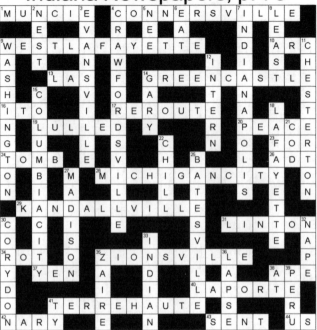

Bizarre Indiana, p. 80

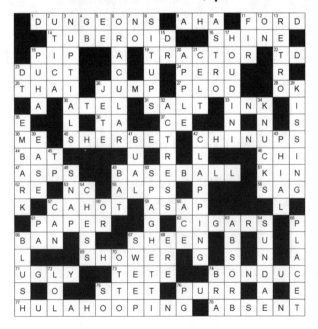

Made in Indiana, p. 83

```
T N E Y Z Q Q X U G J V L R Q S N X H W O U Q U H P J M C Y
A N W J J L Y S P H L C H O M E F R E E Z E R S T C O N S A
X Y I B R P F Q V I P K O A O N V L B I X K R E P C J A V M
V O M E B B H R I U N K M W G I X P O Z Z U V N A T Z H V F
L Y N J J G Q M P C T S E W L G X U G D B Y I I I G A L I J
D G A Z C T W Y S Q U I R F B N D K K B E U W G A U Y H R Z
F S L U T L S E L X P E E D B E Z P E U V N H N O W O P M I
T C E M A M H Q P A A I F L A T A R O U Y A U E U U Z S E S
P J E M P B T Z M Z B R Z Q F G N U O P O M L S K P U I D
R U U T D R E C R E A T I O N A L V E H I C L E S F A K R W
O K R Q T O C R Z K S U D D S R B L V R X I H S Q H L Q T D
V G A I E C B A T D H P G K P C I I A Y Z O O E W J U V M S
U V J E P E M S R S T N E M U R T S N I L A C I S U M X S W
J C Y H M S A C U E Y T R S G I I F D S D B P E D C H I E N J
S T D G Z S V Z C B S E A D O A N D A D G S E I K U N B P M
Z J Y J T E F C K N A I T I E R U U B G U P T M C Y U S L Y
K W K T P D N G B E I Y E M K N D T T M K I F E W L M L A T
L L E L E C T R O N I C R E S I S T O R S H H S E Z P A S I
P V A F M O F Q D N B X S D O L K Q Q M U C I R D L R C T N
K P N U E R U T I N R U F E C I F F O D O O W O S M O I I P
Z H T R T N U W E Y V K Q E D T S O C Z S T I T O N D T C G
I V M X A P L K S O I U O N B C N Y D L P A A Y C U U P P
O K I C L R S S G N I R A E B L L A B N Y T M V B W C E R H
T T N W D O O U E P T M O V F V N G D N C O X E E O T C O V
H A T R O D W P M T I G X O D C P V J P T P N L A P S A D A
S Q M H O U S E H O L D V I D E O E Q U I P M E N T A M U U
D P H Q R C N K A X B P C X U B I K V H K K Y D O T G R C L
Z I U X S T P S H H K A J N I F Q X Q J N P G H I Z R A T J
W F F C W S P O M E O K X U C G I N U F M R L J L N H H S S
U X B X Z C Q A P X W G C J D W B J E L K K I C L O L P V V
```

Indiana Crime and Punishment, p. 84

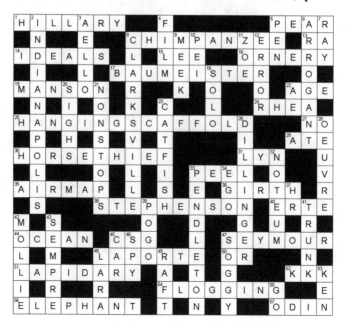

Indiana Crosswords

Bibliography and Recommended Reading List

I would recommend to anyone interested in learning more about the state of Indiana to visit **www.enjoyindiana.com** and request the state's free annual *Indiana Travel Guide*. The book is informative, easy-to-use and full of beautiful photography.

For a great day full of Hoosier information and fun, visit the Indiana State Museum in the White River State Park in downtown Indianapolis: **www.indianamuseum.com.**

Another great resource for information about the Hoosier state is the Indiana Historical Society, also located in downtown Indianapolis: **www.indianahistory.org.**

Books

Berry, Skip and Jolene Phelps Ketzenberger. *The Insider's Guide to Greater Indianapolis*. Manteo, SC: The Insider's Guide, Inc., 1996.

Cavinder, Fred D. *The Indiana Book of Records, Firsts and Fascinating Facts*. Bloomington, IN: Indiana University Press, 1985.

Couch, Ernie and Jill. *Indiana Trivia*. Nashville, TN: Rutledge Hill Press, 1997.

Gisler, Margaret. *Fun With the Family in Indiana*. Old Saybrook, CT: The Globe Pequot Press, 1998.

Keller, Charles E. and Timothy C. Keller. *Birds of Indianapolis*. Bloomington, IN: Indiana University Press, 1993.

Price, Nelson. *Legendary Hoosiers: Famous Folk from the State of Indiana*. Indianapolis, IN: Guild Press of Indiana, 2001.

Nye, Charlie. *Hoosier Century*. Champaign, IL: Sports Publishing, 1999.

Pohlen, Jerome. *Oddball Indiana*. Chicago, IL: Chicago Review Press, 2002.

Thomas, Phyllis. *Off the Beaten Path: Indiana.* Old Saybrook, CT: The Globe Pequot Press, 1998.

Websites with Helpful Information about Indiana (and other places too)

High school sports and team information: **www.ihsaa.org**
Indiana burial sites: **www.findagrave.com**
Indiana business: **www.state.in.us**
Indiana movies: **www.whenmovieweremovies.com**
Indiana tourism: **www.enjoyindiana.com**
Indiana vital statistics: **www.50states.com**
Indy Racing: **www.indy500.com**
Information about Museums in Indiana:
www.museumca.org
James Whitcomb Riley: **www.underthesun.cc**
Quick facts from the U.S. Census Bureau:
www.quickfacts.census.gov